CREATIVE PATCHWORK

Crescent Books · New York

Editors Liz Goodman, Susan Joiner
Text compiled by Stephanie Miller
Consultant Doris E. Marston
Designed by Amelia Edwards

Photographers
Balmer pages 69–80
Michael Boys pages 6 (right), 18, 22 (top left),
56–57
Roger Charity page 87
Mrs. Frere Cook page 8 (right top and bottom)
Alan Duns page 83
Roger Gain page 96
Steve Herr pages 1, 6 (left), 25, 39, 40 (top),
43, 50 (inset), 56
Chris Lewis page 11
Spike Powell page 56 (top)
Ruth Rutter page 85
Bruce Scott page 81
Tubby pages 40 (lower), 53, 59
Michael James Ward pages 50, 60, 86
Peter Watkins page 82
Beta Pictures page 90
Camera Press pages 22 (top right and
lower), 28–29, 33 (lower), 34, 35, 54, 55, 88
Scoop pages 33 (top), 46–47
Transworld Features page 94 and front cove

Artists
Janet Ahlberg pages 22, 61
Caroline Austin pages 73, 75, 83, 85, 89,
92–93, 95
Janet Chipps page 79
Barbara Firth page 83
Chris Hay pages 62, 63, 64, 65, 66, 67, 68
Janine Kirwan pages 3, 4, 5, 7, 20, 23, 26, 27
Chris Le Gee pages 21, 27, 28, 29, 48, 49, 51,
87, 90–91
Margaret Power pages 16, 36, 40, 41, 44
Sue Richards pages 10, 13, 31, 32, 34, 38, 39,
42, 44, 45, 58

Accessories
page 1 scissors at John Lewis, Oxford
Street, London W1
page 11 sofa and accessories by courtesy of
Maples Ltd. 149 Tottenham Court Road,
London W1
page 25 navy scarf at Fenwicks, Bond Street,
London W1
page 36 dress by Jean Muir for Browns,
25 South Molton Street, London W1
Bracelets from Fenwicks, Bond Street,
London W1
Necklace by Adrian Mann, Princess House,
56 Eastcastle Street, London W1
page 39 plain cushions by John Lewis,
Oxford Street, London W1

Designers
page 8 Patchwork skirt designed and made
by Mrs. E. Mason
Flowery quilt designed and made by
Mrs. Frere Cook
page 9 Waistcoat designed and made by
Mrs. E. Mason

page 15 Trousers designed and made by
Mrs. E. Mason
pages 18–19, 24 (top left), 57, American
quilts from a collection belonging to Mrs.
John Bormann
page 23 Photograph album designed and
made by Frances Ross Duncan
page 25 Dressing gown designed and made
by Mrs. J. D. Speid
page 37 Evening coat designed and made by
Patience Walker
page 39 Clamshell cushion designed and
made by Anita Skjold
page 40 Halter top designed and made by
Stephanie Miller
Tea cosy designed and made by Doris E.
Marston
page 43 Samples by Frances Ross Duncan
page 50 Motifs designed and made by
Alison Barrell
page 56 Quilt supplied by courtesy of
Malcolm (Holdings) Ltd. 184 Walton Street,
London SW3
page 58 Hexagonal box designed and made
by Doris E. Marston
pages 60, 86 Cushions and curtains
photographed at Choses, Sloane Street,
London W1
pages 68–80 American quilts from
The American Museum, Bath
page 81 Quilt from the Victoria and
Albert Museum, London
page 87 Patchwork dress designed and
made by Susan Joiner

About this book

Patchwork is an old friend, as familiar and comfortable as an evening by the fire. But nowadays, this traditional craft has taken on new dimensions and a modern fashion-conscious look is as much within the realm of patchwork as grandmother's bedcover.

We show you how to achieve both. There are plenty of romantic quilts with a country-fresh feel, as well as other things for the home: a tea cosy, cushions, wall hangings, even curtains. And there's clothing ranging from super-sophisticated evening wear to a casual jacket. There are bright things to make for your man or your children, plus all sorts of accessories. Never before has there been a patchwork book with so many colour pages full of so many new ideas.

The most ambitious patchwork is really easy with our step-by-step methods, and you'll be surprised at how quickly the work grows and changes with each gem-like patch. The patterns you build can be as intricate or simple as you please; an entire section of this book is devoted to some of the hundreds of traditional designs for you to copy or alter, or to serve as inspiration for your own original pattern.

Patchwork is a living, dynamic thing—a touching way of preserving the memories of a lifetime: a favourite dress or shirt, your first kitchen curtains, all find their way into your work, side by side, like landmarks on a road map. The possibilities are endless, and no two people will ever combine the same materials in the same way—your creation will truly be one of a kind. You are limited only by the breadth of your imagination and the depth of your scrap basket.

Let this beautiful book, a collector's piece in its own right, reacquaint you with the most individualistic and satisfying of crafts.

CONTENTS

CREATIVE PATCHWORK

introducing patchwork

Patchwork is an unashamedly sentimental craft which from its origins has been connected with sharing and neighbourliness, particularly in America. 'Friendship Quilts' were made to commemorate a special occasion, to honour a hero, or to help a family who were down on their luck, or were going West to start a new life.

Each neighbour would give a block, either pieced or decorated with appliqué, and they would all meet to join and quilt the blocks into a finished quilt. Sometimes a particular theme, such as animals, flowers or a family history was decided on and then it was called an 'Album Quilt'. If presented at a ceremony it was called a 'Presentation Quilt'.

'Freedom Quilts' were only made for young men. On a man's 21st birthday young girls of his acquaintance were invited to his house. They spent the afternoon before the celebration supper stitching the quilt top together.

It was then put away until the time came to add it to the others in his future wife's bottom drawer.

'Signature Quilts' were a recognized way of raising money for charity. Usually made from 3-inch squares, the patches were 'sold'; the purchaser's name was written with indelible ink or embroidered on to the patch which was then worked into the quilt.

The 'Marriage Quilt' was the last and most splendid of the thirteen quilts an engaged girl was required to have in America around 1700. The superstition grew that it was bad luck for the girl to work on her own marriage quilt so the girl-friends of the bride each brought a block, usually appliquéd, to her house. They stitched them together and quilted the top and finally gave the quilt to the girl for her wedding present.

A small piece of patchwork made of autographed patches turned into a cushion can still make a charming momento of a wedding, anniversary or special occasion.

From a mixture of plain and small flowered pattern fabrics cut 3 inch squares or 2 inch x 3 inch rectangles. Use the plain fabrics for the signatures written and then embroidered, and join them in a 'Hit and Miss' fashion with the floral patches.

Patchwork grew from domestic economy, from the days when every scrap of material had a value and was saved, to be sewn to another scrap and another, to form fabric for clothing and covering. From these humble beginnings real art emerged, as women used their needles to express themselves. The rags became rich and colourful displays of intricately stitched, interlocking shapes.

Today the art of patchwork is having a great revival. Not because there is really a practical need, but because it still has the same attractions. Centuries ago, patchwork provided the wives of early American settlers with an activity that could be simple and restful or creatively stimulating and amazingly complex. Today, patchwork still provides a means for relaxation and for exercising artistic talent.

Of all popular crafts patchwork is unique in that it can be worked in a wide variety of materials and has instant effect. Beautiful and useful things can be made in a pleasurable and satisfying way.

The history of patchwork

A complete history of patchwork has yet to be written, but its age has been established from discoveries, made by explorers, of both patchwork and appliqué in India, Egypt and other Eastern countries. The modern fashion for leather patchwork may not seem so new when you realize that the oldest piece in the world, a funeral pall made in Egypt three thousand years ago, is in gazelle hide!

As soon as man began to clothe himself and furnish his dwelling it is reasonable to suppose that the bits left over from shaping a skin would have been joined to make a further garment.

When weaving was first invented and cloth was regarded as something new and precious, the need to preserve it was obvious. Patchwork and appliqué both developed in this way – from a need, literally, to patch. Holes could be covered decoratively with appliqué and new garments or covers made from pieces of leftover material.

In time, patchwork spread into all the countries round the Mediterranean and across Europe into England. It is believed to have been introduced by the Crusaders who no doubt saw it in their travels. There are pictures of banners and tunics in many medieval manuscripts which indicate a knowledge of patchwork and appliqué.

There is a large gap in the history of early English patchwork and it was not until the 17th century, when the importing of cottons from India began, that the collection of work began to build up. From then onwards patchwork was done as much for pleasure as from necessity and it began to play a definite part in social life, particularly of the more leisured middle classes.

Although the majority of patchwork was made into bedcovers and quilts, often involving the craft of quilting, furnishings of various kinds and garments were also made. The most productive period of English patchwork lies between the latter half of the 18th and the middle of the 19th centuries. There are many beautiful examples of patchwork, combining good technique and an inspired sense of colour and pattern far removed from the original roughly shaped pieces of cloth from which patchwork began.

The earliest sewing machine was made in 1830 and by 1869 machines were being made for domestic use. The Industrial Revolution was responsible for a decrease in handsewing and in craftwork generally. However, patchwork for decorative use only became fashionable in the late Victorian and Edwardian periods, in less durable forms like crazy-work and Suffolk puffs.

During the two World Wars of the 20th century, patchwork reverted to its original purpose of thrift. People had little time for creativity and used pieces of fabric to 'make do and mend'.

Nowadays our daily lives are full of colour and pattern. Patchwork has been given new vitality by the wide selection of colours and fabrics that are readily available in the shops. It is an exciting revival with endless potential for creative work.

The story of patchwork in North America is a complete one and many books have been written about it. It has, in fact, been said that the history of America is written in its patchwork quilts, for the craft has been part of home and social life ever since the first settlers from Europe established their homes on the east coast of America. It is still a widely practiced and well-loved craft, especially in country areas. The women who sailed from England and Holland to America so long ago, took not only their possessions but their skills, and in exploring the story of American patchwork it is intriguing to find the traditional patterns and colours that appear in work from the countries of origin.

In those early days of America the history of patchwork was repeated, for there was need to be careful with what one had. Further supplies from Europe took a long time to arrive, journeys across the Atlantic were hazardous, thriftiness with materials was imperative. Conditions of life and cold winters were important factors in establishing quilting and patchwork as a means of providing warm covers and clothing.

We are apt to regard the 'sewing bees' and quilting parties which we read about in books of the period as peculiarly American, but in England too, in the past and present, work was shared by families or groups, in areas where a tradition existed. Jane Austen helped in the making of a quilt with her mother and sisters. Even in fairly recent years in the north of England, it was possible to find in the vestry of the village church, or a large room in a house a quilt, patchwork or otherwise, set up on its frame, so that as time or inclination allowed women could go in and work at it.

It is hardly surprising that so pleasant and worthwhile a tradition should have been taken to a new country. 'Quilting picnics' are a great feature of the State Fairs in the rural areas of America and many have their own quilters' magazines – small intimate publications which provide a centre for the exchange of ideas, patterns and instructions between members.

Today quilt patterns appear frequently in the larger American magazines and often include full details of materials, yardage and colour schemes as well as the template shapes needed. American women still take great pride in their quilts like their forebears. Not so long ago a girl did not regard herself as being properly engaged for marriage until she had made her 'baker's dozen' of quilts. The last of the pile was of course the most special – the marriage quilt.

Hundreds of designs were evolved and handed down over the centuries and most of these are current patterns for quilters. The traditional block and all over one-patch patterns each having their own name can be found among the illustrations of books on American patchwork. Each stands for some historical occasion, a family or social event or tradition – perhaps a tribute to some outstanding personality. A visit to the American Museum at Claverton near Bath, England, will show that the appliqué designs are the most popular, though some of the quilts on display are a mixture of applied work and patchwork.

While the word 'patchwork' in America is usually taken to mean 'quilt', the English have always preferred to invent their own designs and to extend the use of patchwork to a wide variety of things.

Creating an individual design, working out a special colour scheme is at the very heart of the fascination of patchwork. The vitality of the patchwork revival in this century is reflected in the glowing colours and exciting patterns seen in contemporary work. Patchwork today is not restricted to the traditional geometric shapes – free shapes can be most exciting. Imaginative and original designs with fabrics have elevated needlework to an art form.

patchwork techniques

Patchwork is still mainly a home craft – sewn throughout by hand using the traditional, centuries-old methods. It was inevitable that the invention of the sewing machine should inspire attempts to use it for patchwork, but until recently nothing more than modern designs in large rectangular pieces had been produced. The invention of the swing needle and machines capable of embroidery have made more complicated techniques possible.

For the great majority who want to do patchwork, hand sewing is the most convenient and pleasurable. You can pick it up at any time, doing a few patches or a little planning as the mood takes you.

Sewing

Patchwork is within the scope of anyone who can sew by hand and knows how to oversew, hem and tack neatly.

Tools

You probably have most of the things that are needed already in your sewing equipment, but since the sewing must be fine and fairly close, needles and threads must be fine too. No needles should be coarser than size 7. Use the finest sewing thread that is available. Pins must be fine too. You could use dressmakers' pins, but tiny short pins, like 'lillikins' or 'lills', are better because they do not get in the way so much. They are particularly useful for stabbing through a patch to hold it in place on a board when planning. A board or small table is invaluable when designing the arrangement of your patchwork. You can use it to lay out patches like a jig-saw. The 'board' can be anything into which pins can easily be stabbed. Cork matting, thick cardboard, insulation board or a card table are all good.

Paper

The patches are generally constructed over paper shapes which are cut out from templates to help make the patches exact. They act as linings and hold the patches out firmly so they may be joined together conveniently. Both tackings and linings are removed when patchwork is completed.

Paper for this purpose can be of any colour but must be of good quality – standard note-paper would do, crisp enough for the edges to be felt within the folds as the edges of the patches are turned. Here again you can be thrifty and use up envelopes, letters, Christmas cards, etc. When heavier types of material are used, then a thin card is necessary. Vilene or Pellon can be used as an alternative and is usually left in, to add firmness.

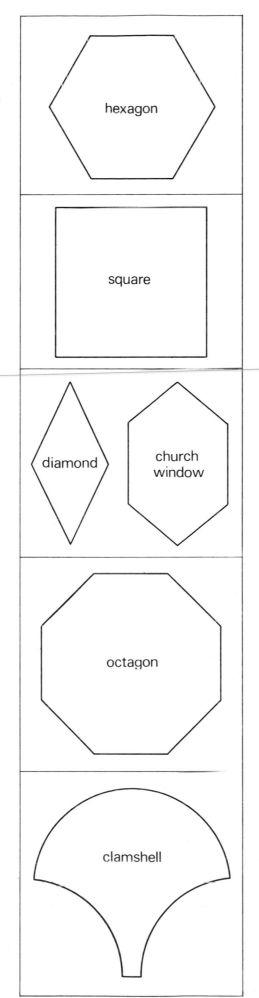

Templates

The word 'template' means pattern and in patchwork these are the patterns for the patches. There is a variety of shapes. The most popular come in a great assortment of sizes, of which the hexagon, diamond and square are certainly the commonest. The church window (long hexagon in most catalogues) is another alternative shape. The octagon is not so frequently used and has to be combined with a square of the same size. The clamshell is the usual name given to the mushroom-like shape which creates attractive scalloped lines when the patches are joined. It is also called 'shell' or 'scale'. You will find the basic template shapes appearing in many other crafts and in unsuspected places, such as glazing, mosaics and parquetting. In modern architecture the hexagonal shape is frequently used as a room shape as it is attractive and space-saving. In fact once you are interested, you will discover patchwork patterns in everything.

Templates may be home-made from card, plastic or metal or they can be bought from craft suppliers. Either way it is essential that they are accurate otherwise the patches will never fit together precisely. Plastic or metal templates are best because they keep their rigidity. Card templates will not last very long and soon lose their accuracy.

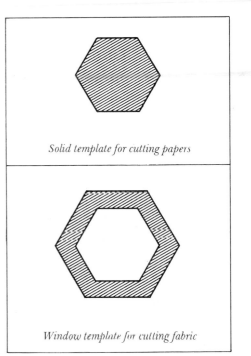

Solid template for cutting papers

Window template for cutting fabric

Templates bought from a craft shop are often pre-packaged. They usually supply a solid metal shape, together with a slightly larger plastic one with a frosted band round the clear area. The latter is the 'window' from which the patch is cut; the solid is the pattern for the papers. If the solid shape can be bought separately, then the window may be home-made. Draw the solid shape very accurately on to card. Measure $\frac{1}{4}$-inch all round the outline to make a larger replica of the shape. Finally cut out both outlines with a scalpel or modelling knife and you will find that you have your own window template.

The size of the shape is usually given as the length of one of its sides. For example a $\frac{1}{2}$-inch diamond or hexagon has sides of that measurement. Beginners could practice with a $\frac{7}{8}$-inch or 1-inch hexagon. The square is also comparatively easy, but the turnings which lie alongside the corners can be tiresome. Only the top edges are stitched when joining up and these turnings can get in the way.

Using the templates

The solid template represents the size of the patch when it has been made. Use it to cut out the paper backings.

Trim off a strip of paper a little wider than the template, fold it two or three times into a pad and place the metal in the centre. Hold it firmly in one hand, then cut round with sharp scissors, placing the blades close to the metal edges, to be sure of accuracy.

Cut the fabric to size with the window template. Place the window on the fabric then draw round the outer edge with a pencil or chalk. Cut out the patch along the pencilled line.

Pin the paper shape to the wrong side of the patch. Turn in the $\frac{1}{4}$-inch overlap of material all round and tack down with neatly folded corners until the shape is completed. Pinch the folds in to make sure the material fits the paper lining exactly.

The sharp points of a diamond patch need a double fold because of the extra material. The clamshell has a different, more compli-

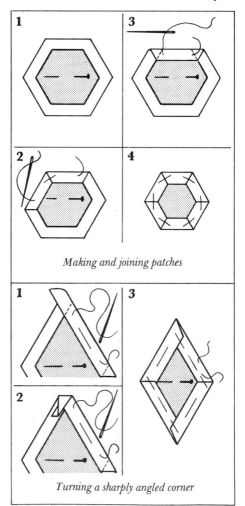

Making and joining patches

Turning a sharply angled corner

cated technique from the other shapes. Clamshells are usually joined by hemming, rarely with oversewing. The scalloped arrangements are attractive but because they are difficult to make and assemble they are less popular than the more usual patches.

Materials for patchwork

Generally speaking the best materials for patchwork are those which do not fray or stretch, and are firm in weave and texture. Good cottons head the list from all points of view. Man-made materials on the whole are not as easy to use as those made from natural fibres, because of their crease resisting qualities. And of course leather has once more come into its own.

Always observe two important rules when selecting materials for a piece of work. Never mix silks and cottons and only combine materials of equal weight and thickness. There is one sad lady who made herself a patchwork bedspread and mixed cotton print and corduroy together. The finished patchwork would never lie flat as the fabrics were of such different weights and to add to the disastrous consequences, the colour ran when the cover was washed! If you are in any doubt test for colour fastness before beginning the work. Patchwork is often made into things which need to be washed and if the colours run they could ruin something into which you have put a great deal of effort.

Silks and drip dry cottons are marked permanently by pin and needlemarks. To avoid this, the paper must be held in the middle of the wrong side and the tacking stitched only into the paper, not right through the patch. Practise this on materials which do not need this care.

Fabrics can be mixed in patchwork and look very effective but it is better to confine mixtures to things that will not receive hard wear. Silks and velvets or silks and tweeds look very rich but in wear the stronger fabric will tend to make the weaker one pull out.

The difference in weight between two materials can be minimized by using a bonded fabric lining with the lighter fabric.

Designing in patchwork

The excellence of any piece of patchwork depends equally on good technique and good colour and design. This is true of even the smallest piece of work. A window template is particularly useful when using a patterned material. It means you can select the exact units you need to make your own arrangement. Texture can be very important, it is the extra factor which can add interest and light and shade to plain colours. It is wise to consider the grain of the material, for its direction can matter a great deal in creating the desired effect.

Take time over planning your design. It can be the most absorbing and enjoyable stage before you really embark on joining patches together. As they are made, use them like pieces of a jig-saw on the table or mat, shift and change their arrangement until you find a satisfactory one. This is your

jumping off place and you can then go ahead and sew.

Begin by taking two patches and placing them with right sides together. Oversew finely and closely along one edge, taking up only two or three threads from each fold into every stitch. Do not take in the paper inside. When the join is completed flatten the seam and carry on sewing together the rest. Do this by making up groups or units. Then join these, and repeat the process until the required area is complete for what you have planned. If you are a beginner be content at first to make something small and quick. There's a variety of articles to choose from that involve only simple designs and enable you to master the various techniques before graduating to larger, more demanding patchwork. Pin cushions, balls, belts, spectacle cases and bags are recommended for the elementary stage. Cushions and cosies, border decorations and motifs for curtains, aprons or box tops, enable us to cope later with more extensive articles which call for greater skill in designing.

Colour schemes

A good design is generally a basically simple one, perhaps using only two main colours. It's fun to work it out in shades and tints. Random schemes can be very pretty, especially if some sorting and grouping of colour is attempted. A jumble of many colours can never have the character of a carefully chosen and well-balanced colour scheme worked out in plain and patterned fabrics. Careful preparation is extremely important. If you are a flower arranger, if you are an artist, or have any practice at all in the use of colour, you will realize this and be able to apply your previous knowledge.

Finishing patchwork

The tackings and papers are all removed when the patches have been joined. The finishing-off stage has been reached – edges may need to be straightened by inserting half patches, or strips may be placed behind to fill spaces or strengthen curves. Here you must use common sense and choose the best method for the particular job in hand. The work needs to be lined to strengthen and neaten, once straightened edges must be bound, piped or corded to give a good finish. Pads or fillings for cushion covers and tea or coffee cosies should be thought about in the early stages and planned beforehand. Choose whatever finish seems most suitable – remembering shape and practical use.

When all is done, when you have made something you can look on with pride, you can derive a good deal of satisfaction from knowing that you have used scraps which might never have otherwise been used: yet out of them you will have created something beautiful and useful. For in patchwork, you not only develop a certain amount of technical skill and benefit from the relaxation of handsewing, but also have the unique experience of expressing your own personality in colour and design.

machine patchwork

The invention of the swing needle sewing machine has made machine patchwork a speedy alternative to hand stitching, especially if you are working with patches of 1½ inch and over in length. (This is measured along the side of the patch, not the overall length.) Smaller patches are better sewn by hand.

Many fabrics are suitable for machine-made patchwork, particularly cottons and wools, silks, needlecord and velvets and fine tweeds. Very densely woven fabrics are not suitable for machine patchwork if you are making patches with acute angles, like diamonds, as the needle has to cope with several thicknesses of fabric.

Leather, suede and PVC coated fabrics are particularly good as they will not fray and so not need turnings. You simply cut the patches to size without an allowance for seams, butt the edges of the patches together and swing stitch them on the right side.

Sewing the patches together
Prepare the patches as for hand sewing. If the patchwork is for fashion appliqué use bonded fibre fabric instead of papers and leave them in the finished work.

Needles, threads and stitches
Use a No. 14 machine needle (continental No. 90) and change to a new needle more often, as patchwork papers tend to blunt the point. Stitch with a fine thread, No. 50 or 60, and use a mercerized cotton, like Sylko, or synthetic thread according to the material you are using.

Choose a suitable thread colour. A white thread looks well on mixed colours, or match the thread to one of the basic colours in the fabric. It is important to keep the same colour and type of thread throughout the work.

On swing needle machines the 'swing' of the stitch (that is, the stitch width) can be adjusted in the same way as the stitch length. As a general guide for machine patchwork, select a swing of 1½ to 2 and a medium stitch length. Loosen the top tension a little.

It will be necessary to adjust the controls slightly according to the fabric and length of the patch. For instance, a 3-inch hexagon will need the stitches further apart than a 2-inch hexagon although the swing will remain the same.

For the best results experiment with your machine, trying out the stitches on folded scraps of fabric.

Place two patches together with the right sides facing. Make sure that they match evenly but allow the underneath patch to show just a fraction along the working edge. This way you will be able to see that the stitches are penetrating both patches.

A swing needle swings from left to right and back again. Left is the starting point and you must always start the needle ready to swing to the left. Turn the balance wheel by hand to discover which way the needle is going to swing and set it ready to swing to the left.

Place the patches under the machine needle and turn the balance wheel towards you so that the needle pierces the top right hand corner of the pair of patches. Lower the presser foot and stitch, not too quickly at first.

At the left hand swing the needle should pierce the fabric and papers of the two patches and at the right hand swing the needle should pass just beyond the side of the patches.

When you come to the end of the working edge, make sure that the needle swings to the right for the last stitch – you will then be ready to swing back to the starting point when you begin the next seam. Give the balance wheel a half turn towards you, lift the presser foot and draw out the patch, leaving at least 2 inches of thread before cutting off. This is essential as the ends must be tied off to secure the stitching. It is best to tie off with a double knot as this prevents the threads becoming tangled.

If you prefer, instead of tying off each pair of patches separately, you can stitch a whole series of pairs of patches together in sequence so long as you leave enough thread between them for tying off. The threads are cut afterwards.

When stitching diamond patches it may be necessary with some fabrics to 'help' the machine over the points as there can be up to eight layers of material to penetrate. Open out each seam and you will see that the patches are joined together with firm, even stitches; straight at the front and criss-crossed at the back.

Add as many patches as you need, keeping the grain of the material running as straight as possible.

When the work is large enough, take out the tacking threads and remove the papers. (This will also make it easier to work if the patchwork becomes cumbersome). The papers may have been caught by the needle but will pull away easily, and often can be used again.

Mounting
If you have used bonded fibre fabric instead of papers, leave it in. Catch the bonded fibre fabric to the patchwork occasionally and mount the patchwork on to the garment by stitching round the edges with tiny hem stitches.

If the area of appliquéd patchwork is large, catch it to the fabric of the garment occasionally.

Pressing
Machine patchwork should be pressed well, with a steam iron and a pressing cloth. If there is velvet in the patchwork use a needleboard. Press as if it were hand-sewn patchwork and pay particular attention to the edges of the piece if the patchwork is for fashion appliqué.

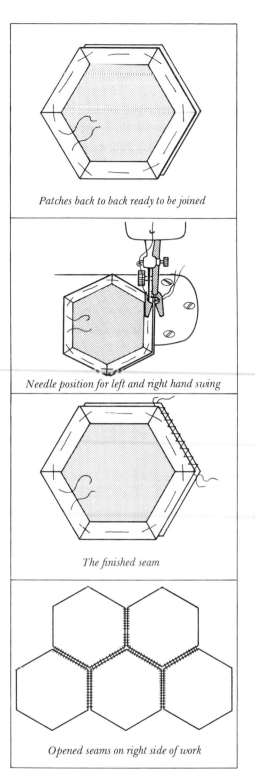

Patches back to back ready to be joined

Needle position for left and right hand swing

The finished seam

Opened seams on right side of work

Lining
Although patchwork makes a strong fabric if it is properly stitched and tied off, it is easily distorted because the grain of the fabric used in the patches does not always run in the same direction. Because of this it is necessary to line patchwork that is to be used in large pieces for making up garments. The lining fabric then acts as a strengthening base and will take the strain instead of the patchwork.

To line patchwork, place it on the lining fabric, wrong sides facing, and catch the two together at regular intervals (every two patches or so) with tiny stitches. Tack round the edges and then treat the lined patchwork as if it were a single layer of fabric.

hexagons

If you are experimenting with your first piece of patchwork the hexagon with six equal sides is by far the simplest shape.

The wide angles at the corners mean that there is no difficult folding of the fabric as with the long diamond or triangle. Seven hexagons joined together make a single rosette: by making one rosette you can learn all the basic techniques of patchwork. A 'hexagon' has been used here to make a simple table mat but you could make a pin-cushion with a smaller template or sew a rosette to the pocket of an apron or dress or join several rosettes together to make a small cushion cover.

First use the template to cut seven paper shapes from stiff paper. These will be the size of the finished patch and it is most important that they are cut out accurately. If you have a 'window' template use this to cut out the patches of fabric. If not, allow $\frac{3}{8}$ inch round the basic template for turnings.

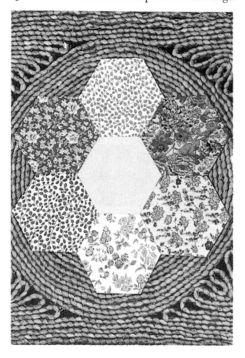

It is best to have two edges of the template parallel to the straight grain of the fabric. Choose a firm, pure cotton fabric for your first attempt. It is possible to use velvets, silks and lurex fabrics but they are more difficult to handle. Do not mix fabrics of different weights and if you are using old and new fabrics together wash the new material first in case it shrinks later. Always iron out all creases before working. If the material is so transparent that the turnings show through, use a vilene lining instead of a paper one, and leave it in the finished patch.

The mat is made in fine lawn in various small floral designs in closely related pastel shades. As you get more experienced in the design of patchwork you will learn how to achieve

different effects with colour, tone and textures but to begin with it is best to avoid harsh contrasts or large violent patterned fabric.

The patches are made by pinning the paper patch to the wrong side of the material, then folding over the turnings and tacking round the patch using one stitch to secure each corner. Finish off with a small extra stitch and take out the pin.

To join the patches place two right-sides together and with tiny even stitches oversew along one edge. Fasten off firmly by working backwards for four stitches. Join a third patch into the angle made by the first two patches. Continue sewing the patches together until you have completed the rosette.

When all the patches are sewn together the patchwork should be pressed on the wrong side with a warm iron. If the right side of the work needs pressing remove all the tacking stitches but leave the papers in so the turnings do not leave a mark. Press gently on the right side before removing the papers. Tack round the outside edge of the rosette to prevent turnings from fraying. Place rosette on lining fabric and trace round with a sharp pencil cutting the lining $\frac{3}{8}$ inch larger than the rosette. Turn in facing, clipping the angles and oversew the edge to finish neatly. Remove tacking.

If you are mounting the rosette on to another fabric, pin the patchwork into place and, using tiny stitches, slip stitch all round. Remove tackings and press lightly to finish.

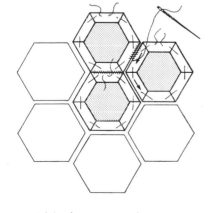

Joining hexagons to make a rosette

Early quilts made in regular hexagons were called 'mosaic' or 'honeycomb'. The rosette form developed because it is a pretty way of using up quite small quantities of fabric without getting involved in an all-over design. It is also easier to work in small units.

Names like 'Grandmother's Flower Garden' and 'French Bouquet' were used to describe American quilts which consisted of a single rosette, representing the flower, with a second row of hexagons in a printed green fabric to represent the foliage. These double rosettes were then joined by white or calico hexagons representing the 'paths'.

An easy version of this can be made by buying enough quilted pique fabric in white or natural to cover your bed. Make single or double rosettes and sew to the quilt at regular intervals, make a border of hexagons and half-hexagons to make an effective edging. Other ways of making a quilt are to sew rosettes in a border round the edge or to link the rosettes with a swag of single patches.

When planning a border design like the 'ocean waves' skirt border, you must be sure that you have enough of each fabric to complete the design.

Grandmother's Flower Garden quilt with yellow centres to each double rosette

Simple placemat, made by forming a rosette of hexagons (opposite page)

7

Spotted, striped and checked cotton were used to make the ocean wave skirt (left). To get the best effect, the fabrics should be of different tonal values, shading from light to dark. The same fabrics but smaller templates were used to make the single rosettes which were slipstitched to the skirt

In the modern flowery quilt (above) the skilful choice of floral chintz fabrics make a charming flower garland design. When planning a design of this kind a window template is a help

Care should be taken in arranging the patches so that the flowers and leaves are to scale and look realistic

To make the child's waistcoat (right), buy a simple pattern. Make a length of patchwork, press well and carefully remove papers. Lay the pattern on the patchwork and machine stitch side and shoulder seams. Baste ⅜-inch single turning to inside all round waistcoat and armholes. Press. Cut out lining, stitch side and shoulder seams and hem neatly to waistcoat and armhole edges

squares and rectangles

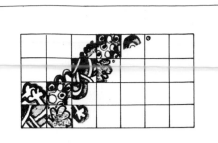

Hit and miss arrangement of square patches

Hit and miss rectangles (above and right)

The square as a patchwork shape looks deceptively simple. It is the easiest patch to cut as you simply use the grain of the material as a guide for cutting the straight lines. However, no other shape looks so obviously inaccurate if the four sides are not exactly the same length and the corners not exactly right-angled.

Squares came very early in the development of patchwork. After the first 'crazy' patchwork made from random scraps of fabric, the women began to arrange the scraps into patterns and designs. The simplest shapes were squares and rectangles and these were sewn together in a 'hit and miss' pattern of alternating light and dark fabrics. A slightly more sophisticated pattern is 'brick wall' which as its name implies consists of rectangular patches of different shades sewn together like a brick wall. These designs are all known as 'one-patch' – that is an all-over design made from the same repeated unit.

If you are using a one-patch design to make a bedcover, or even a cushion, it is well worth planning it carefully beforehand. Mark out the pattern on graph paper and use felt-tip pens to fill in the colours, or use the coloured pages of magazines to cut out the shapes. Ruth Finley, in her book 'Old Patchwork Quilts', says, "Let no one imagine that these all-over one patch quilts were easy to design. Such quilts must be comprehended in their entirety rather than by patches or blocks, and therefore they require the eye of a true artist both as regards colour and form."

After the one-patch comes the two-patch – a square or rectangle divided in half diagonally, then the four patch and the nine-patch. More complicated divisions of the square – the five-patch and the seven-patch (a square divided into 49 smaller squares) are also used but are less common as they are so difficult to cut. Some of the early patchworkers must have been enthusiastic amateur mathematicians.

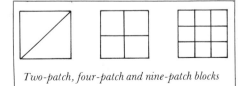

Two-patch, four-patch and nine-patch blocks

Provided the patches are cut accurately and the same width of turning is taken throughout, square patchwork can easily be made on a sewing machine. Large pieces of patchwork fabric can be machined quickly with a straight stitch if the patches are seamed into long strips and then joined together to the required size. If the sequence of patches is planned carefully even quite complicated one-patch designs, such as 'Grandmother's Postage Stamp', can be machine made.

If you are planning to work with a small square it is still best to use a paper shape. The final turn is the most difficult to work when stitching up the patches. The turnings tend to get in the way at the corners. These can be trimmed away slightly. It is a help to do this stitching resting on a firm surface.

Squares can be used diagonally and like this look effective as borders, either appliquéd directly on to the fabric or patched into a strip with triangles. Squares are often used with octagons.

Another method

A strong patchwork fabric can be made with an ordinary sewing machine without making papers if you are working with squares or rectangles. Cut the patches accurately on the straight grain of the fabric. Join right sides together into a strip the required length of the fabric. Make sure you take exactly the same turnings for each join. When you have made the right number of strips to make a wide enough piece join them together, face to face. Press open the seams on the wrong side of the fabric. On the right side carefully top stitch up and down the line of patches $\frac{1}{8}$ inch on either side of the seam.

This is useful for garments such as shirts that need regular washing.

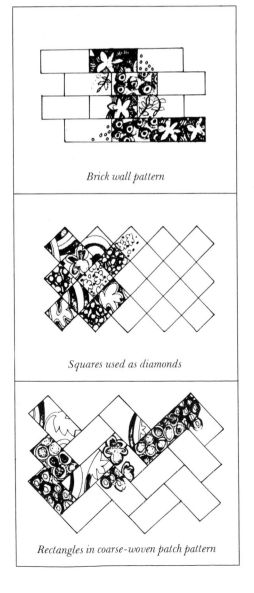

Brick wall pattern

Squares used as diamonds

Rectangles in coarse-woven patch pattern

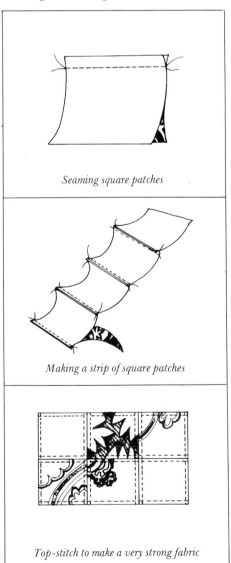

Seaming square patches

Making a strip of square patches

Top-stitch to make a very strong fabric

For the cheerful apron and bag (left), cut out the basic shapes from a paper pattern and sew as given for the jacket and shorts above. In the design shown on the left, a plain fabric has been used for the yoke and hem band of the dress and the top and handles of the bag

Cool and summery short-sleeved jacket and shorts made in squares of machined patchwork (right). To make, buy a paper pattern, make a length of patchwork and press well. Place the pattern on the patchwork and cut out, repeat for the lining. Make up as usual

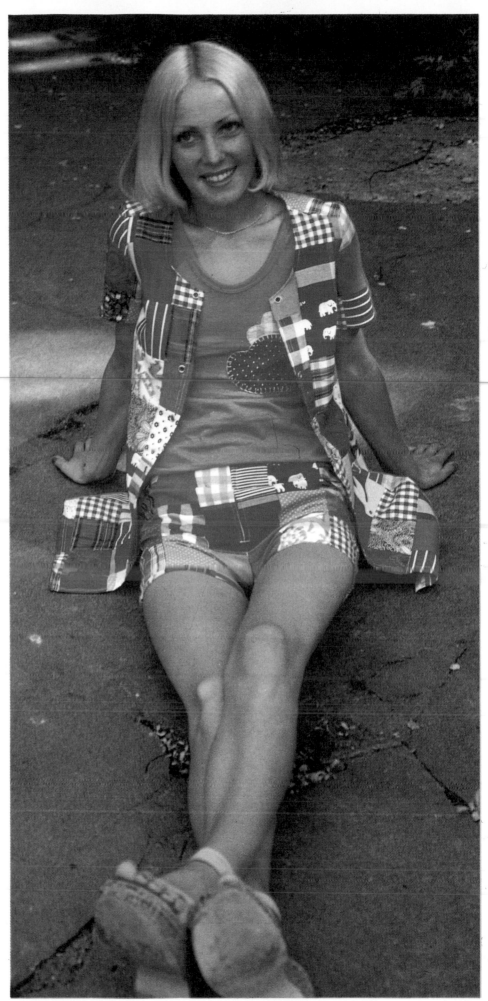

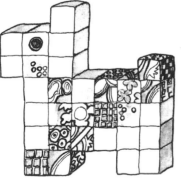

The toy dog (above) is simply made from 92 patchwork squares. You will need 30 for each side and 32 joined together in a strip to make the gusset. Sew the squares together into the toy shape shown and stuff with kapok or foam chips

The charming long skirt for a child (above) is made of 60 4-inch square patches. The skirt is 6 patches long and 10 patches wide. Gather into waistband and insert a 6-inch zip in the centre back seam. Make a hem facing to match the waistband fabric. The girl in our picture is 5 years old

To make the trousers (right) buy a pattern and make a length of patchwork. Press well and remove papers carefully. Place the pattern on patchwork and cut out. Do the same for the lining. Use two strips of plain material for straps if necessary. Make extra patches to lengthen trousers as the child grows

happi coat to make in patchwork squares

Making the Happi coat

The Happi coat, in big, bright patchwork squares, makes an ideal housecoat or beach-coat, and is fairly simple to make. Use cotton fabrics of equal weight for the patchwork, with facing fabric in one of the main colours of the patchwork.

You will need:

A large bag of cotton fabric scraps in different colours and designs

2¾ yards unbleached dress weight calico, for lining

2¼ yards · 36 inch wide navy cotton, for facings.

Make a paper pattern from the graph (one square equals 1 inch) and, using fabric scraps, cut patches approximately 4 inches by 4 inches (although some of the patches in the Happi coat illustrated are oblong). Lay the patchwork pieces out on a table until there are enough to make a Back, two Fronts, two Sleeves and two Pockets, seeing that colours are evenly distributed.

Keep the piles separate. Right sides facing, machine patches together into strips, allowing ½ inch seams throughout. Join strips to make the area of fabric required for each pattern piece.

For the sleeves, make two pieces of patchwork, each 22 inches by 15½ inches. For the back, make one piece, 35½ inches by

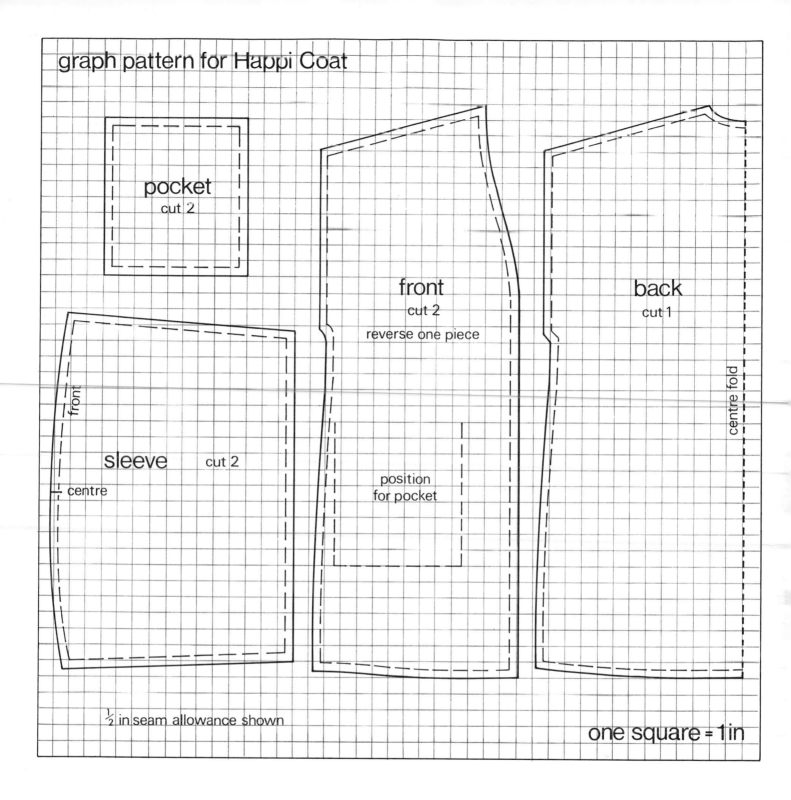

graph pattern for Happi Coat

pocket
cut 2

front
cut 2

reverse one piece

back
cut 1

centre fold

sleeve cut 2

front

centre

position for pocket

½ in seam allowance shown

one square = 1in

26 inches and, for the fronts, two pieces, each 36 inches by 12½ inches. For the pockets, make two pieces, each 9 inches by 8¼ inches. Pin the pattern pieces to the patchwork and cut out one back on the fold, two sleeves, two fronts and two pockets. Pin the paper pattern pieces to the lining fabric and cut out the same pieces. Place one pocket, tack and sew by hand all around. Make the second pocket in the same way and then cut two pocket facings from the navy cotton fabric, each 9 inches by 4 inches. Place one facing edge to the upper edge of one pocket, tack and sew. Turn facing to inside, tuck raw edge under and stitch. Repeat with other pocket. Pin pockets

to coat fronts in positions indicated on the graph. Tack and then machine stitch.

Tack the patchwork fronts to the lining fronts, wrong sides together. Tack and machine stitch the patchwork back only to the fronts along the shoulder seams and down the side seams, working on wrong side. Machine back lining to shoulder seams and hem down side seams. Sew patchwork sleeve seams, with right side to inside, and then, right side to right side, ease sleeves into armholes and pin, tack and sew. Sew sleeve lining side seams, tack into sleeves, wrong side to wrong side, and hem to shoulder seam. Tack lining to patchwork all around the edges of the garment.

Facings

From navy cotton, cutting on the fold where it is convenient, cut one belt, 78 inches by 5 inches, two belt slots, each 3 inches by 2½ inches, two front facings, each 39 inches by 4 inches, one hem, 52 inches by 5 inches, and two cuffs, each 21 inches by 5 inches. Make up the belt slots and stitch in position at the waist.

Pin, tack and sew edge of facing to the edges of the coat, mitring hem and front facings neatly.

Turn facings to wrong side, fold under the raw edges and hand sew to finish. Finish off cuffs in the same way. Make up the belt and pull through the belt slots.

This is a selection of inspiring old American quilts from Georgia

The beautiful double-sided quilt (top left) is a one-patch design made in squares used diagonally and relies heavily on subtle changes of tone for its effect. The whole quilt is bordered with black and quilting stitches run through both thicknesses

In the quilt (left) rectangles cut from contrasting shades of wool are stitched together to make diagonal zig-zag shapes. The strong black and red patches are balanced by the cool beige, blue and grey shades

Another one-patch design (above) of linked squares used as diamonds. The pastel centre of the quilt darkens gradually to the plain red border

In the strip quilt (right) the Hit and Miss four-patch blocks are joined by strips of dark and light blue fabric

triangles and diamonds

Triangles and diamonds are possibly the most popular geometric figures used in quilting.

The Triangle

Two shapes of triangle are used in patchwork – the half-diamond or pyramid and the long triangle.

The pyramid is an isosceles triangle with a short base line and two equal sides. It is made by dividing a hexagon and is often used to make border designs such as 'Streak of Lightning' or 'Dog's Tooth'.

The long triangle is made by halving a diamond lengthwise or dividing a square diagonally. Most early patchwork designs were based on the square and as triangles were the easiest shapes to cut from a square for variation many examples of a square and triangle mixture are found. 'Windmill', 'Old Maid's Puzzle', 'Goose Tracks' and 'Flags' are all examples, and there must be hundreds of others.

When making triangular patches the corners should be folded and tacked as for the diamond.

Triangles can be combined with many other shapes and they are useful for filling in to make a straight edge to the work.

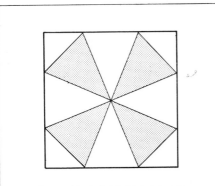

Square block divided into triangles to form the illusion of an octagon

An octagon divided into triangles and joined into a square block with smaller triangles gives a pretty almost-circular effect.

A square folded in half diagonally twice produces four triangles. This design is called 'Cotton Reel' when pairs of light and dark patches are used on either side of the patch. This very simple form of triangular patch was used as a border or made up in strips and sewn together to make an all-over quilt.

'Whirlwind' is a striking four-patch block usually made in two colours, combining half-square triangles and quarter-square triangles and gives the effect of a whirling pin wheel.

The Diamond

The diamond is a popular patchwork shape which looks effective on its own and also combines well with other shapes. There are several diamond shapes but the most common are the diamond or 'lozenge' based on the hexagon and the 'long diamond', based on the square.

It is more difficult to make than the hexagon as the sharply pointed angles require a double fold of material. Great care must be taken, otherwise the finished patch could be bulky and uneven.

When making diamond patches cut out papers and fabric patches as for the hexagon. It is helpful to use fairly thick card when cutting out the papers as it will be a stronger and more accurate guide for the sharp points.

Diamond shapes have a natural bias so when cutting out the material where possible lay the side of the template along the grain of the fabric. This limits the bias to one direction only.

To make up the patch

1 Pin the paper shape carefully to the fabric patch.

2 Fold over the right hand hem first and tack with two stitches to hold the fabric firm.

3 Mitre the corner as shown in the diagram, but do not stitch.

4 Fold over and tack the left hand hem.

This is repeated for the other two sides.

The patches are seamed together with a small even stitch, working from the wide angles of the patch towards the points. This is particularly important when the diamonds are being worked into a star pattern.

A mixture of silks and satins can look beautiful when made into a simple trellis pattern of diamonds but the inexperienced patchworker would be wise to experiment with a soft but closely woven cotton that will seam and fold easily. Velvets and thick fabrics are very difficult to fold into the sharp angles.

The lozenge-shaped diamond is often seen as the three-dimensional box pattern. This consists of diamonds in three different tones – light, medium and dark – sewn together to look like a cube. In America these were known as 'Baby Blocks'. As an all-over pattern this can be quite tiring to look at so it was often confined to borders of quilts. Another popular border was the zig-zag pattern, often using two contrasting colours and this diamond can make a six-point star.

The long diamond is the basis of the 'Star of Bethlehem' design which was a favourite with American needlewomen. The eight points of the star are extended to make a huge star-shape, its proportions suitable for making a double bedcover. Long diamonds are often combined with squares and triangles.

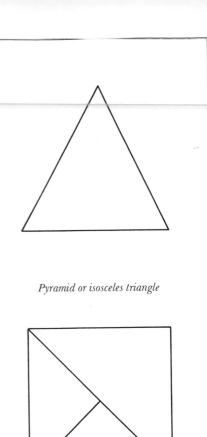

Pyramid or isosceles triangle

Half-square and quarter-square triangles

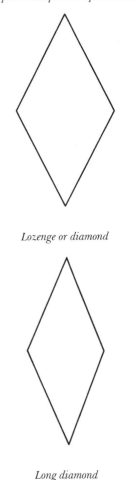

Lozenge or diamond

Long diamond

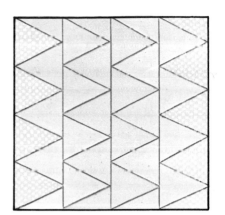

Streak of Lightning

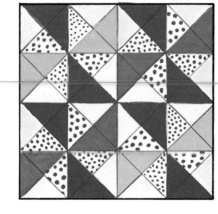

A Thousand Pyramids

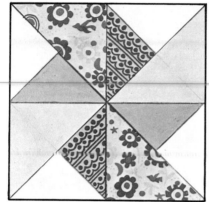

Dog's Tooth

Cotton Reels

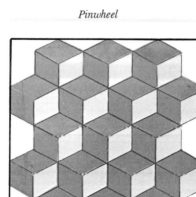

Pinwheel

Whirlwind

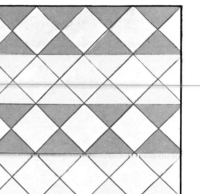

Trellis

Baby's Blocks

Building Blocks effect

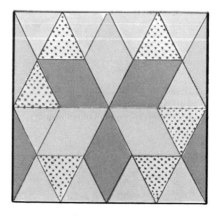

Six-point Star

Eight-point Star

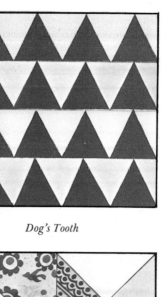

Star of Bethlehem

This design is formed by dividing an octagon
into triangles — making eight
large triangles and by adding four
smaller triangles to each corner to
make a square. Although this is a strictly
geometric design the total effect is
soft and delicate

patchwork album

Choose a photograph album to cover. Try and find one which is held together with cord so it can be dismantled and you can work with the cover only. Decide what is to be your background colour and buy enough material to cover the album. Use $\frac{1}{2}$ yard of 36-inch wide cotton poplin for an average sized album. Use a dark colour so finger marks won't show, unless you want to cover a special wedding or baby album.

Next choose materials for boxes which are made up from three long diamonds. One side should be lighter in colour than the others and, if possible, one should be darker and the other something in between, so the boxes will work in perspective.

Use diamonds with $1\frac{1}{4}$-inch sides and cotton lawn, as the finer the fabric the easier it is to make the pointed corners accurate. Cut out all fabric diamonds with $\frac{1}{8}$-inch seam allowance larger than paper patterns. Tack carefully to the paper patterns and press. Putting right sides together stitch diamonds together using smallest stitches possible. Sew three diamonds together to make boxes. Press each box on both sides. Join boxes together and press again. Remove tacking threads and paper patterns.

Cut out background fabric to size of complete album cover front and back plus $\frac{1}{2}$ inch extra top and bottom for turning and enough material to lap over to wrong side.

Position patchwork on right side of front cover and tack in place. Appliqué on to ground fabric using small hem stitches. Remove tacking threads and press both back and front. Make up cover as follows:

If fabric is not wide enough make a seam at both fold lines.

The finished cover is now ready for the cardboard album cover to slip into. Make eyelet holes in corresponding places to cardboard cover, using a pencil to mark position. Place a small piece of fabric on the wrong side to make a double thickness of fabric for each eyelet hole, cut out hole and strengthen the edges using a button hole stitch worked from right side. Trim spare fabric from wrong side of hole. Press on wrong side.

Bend cover with two right sides facing and slip on patchwork cover. Thread cord through cover and inside pages.

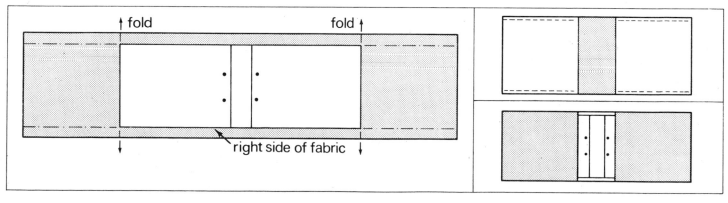

Top left : Star and eight-point stands out vividly against the quilted yellow background of the quilt

Old shirting and dress cottons were used to make this pretty circular tablecloth in faded tones (above)

This skirt (left) is made from suede patches on a swing-needle machine. The patches are sewn together in zig-zag stitch without turnings. Buy a simple, slightly flared skirt pattern and draw the design on it, making sure that the diamonds fit together well at the side seams, and note the colour scheme. Make a duplicate pattern on stiffer paper — mark both shapes and colour. Cut out these diamonds and use them as templates to cut out the suede patches. The original pattern can then be used as a guide for stitching the patches together

This splendid dressing gown is made
entirely of silks and satins.
A bold red satin was used for the front
edging, cuffs and quilted collar. The
front facing is cut to fill in the half
diamond shapes and to make a firm edge
for the concealed zipper fastening. The
entire garment is lined in silk and
interlined.
This is a beautiful example of exquisite
patchwork carefully planned and
skilfully made. When working with silk
and satin, take care to use very fine pins
and needles and thread. A garment
such as this should, of course, be dry
cleaned

other shapes

The Pentagon shape with five equal sides cannot be used without other shapes if it is to be made into a flat patchwork. Twelve equilateral pentagons will automatically make up into a ball.

Another form of pentagon is the diamond with one point removed. Six of these combined with a hexagon will make a pretty tapering star shape.

The Octagon with its eight wide angles is an easy shape to make, but it cannot be joined on all sides without the addition of a square. It is a good shape to begin with as it looks good even in large sizes. You can make an attractive patched fabric with different colours of octagon joined with squares in a constant plain, dark colour. These effectively hold the design together.

The Long Hexagon or Church Window is really a hexagon stretched between two points. It combines well with squares and octagons, but also looks good on its own either in a star formation or simply in rows fitting one into the other.

The Coffin, with its blunted ends is not a popular shape and is usually used alone.

The Rhomboid is a parallelogram adapted from the rectangle. It makes a pleated, three dimensional effect border if light and dark shades are used alternatively. Ready-made templates are not available in this shape so they would have to be cut from strong card. Combined with the square it will make another version of the three-dimensional box pattern. If fabrics of the right tonal value are chosen this can be altered visually into a flight of steps.

The Extended Rectangle, an odd but useful patchwork shape, is used with other shapes as a filling in piece. It can be combined with the octagon and square to make a basket weave effect.

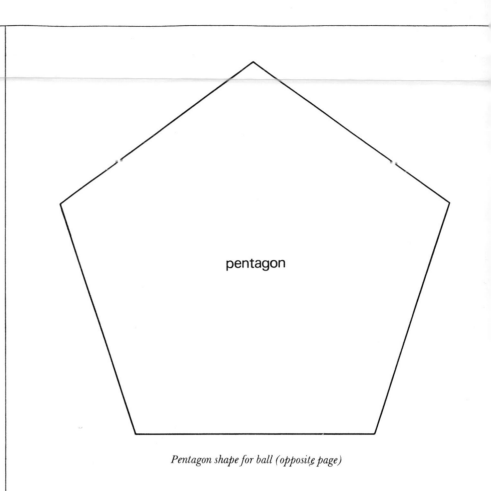

pentagon

Pentagon shape for ball (opposite page)

strip or extended rectangle

adapted rectangle

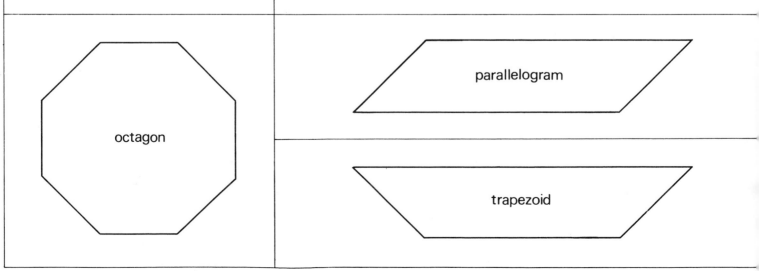

octagon

parallelogram

trapezoid

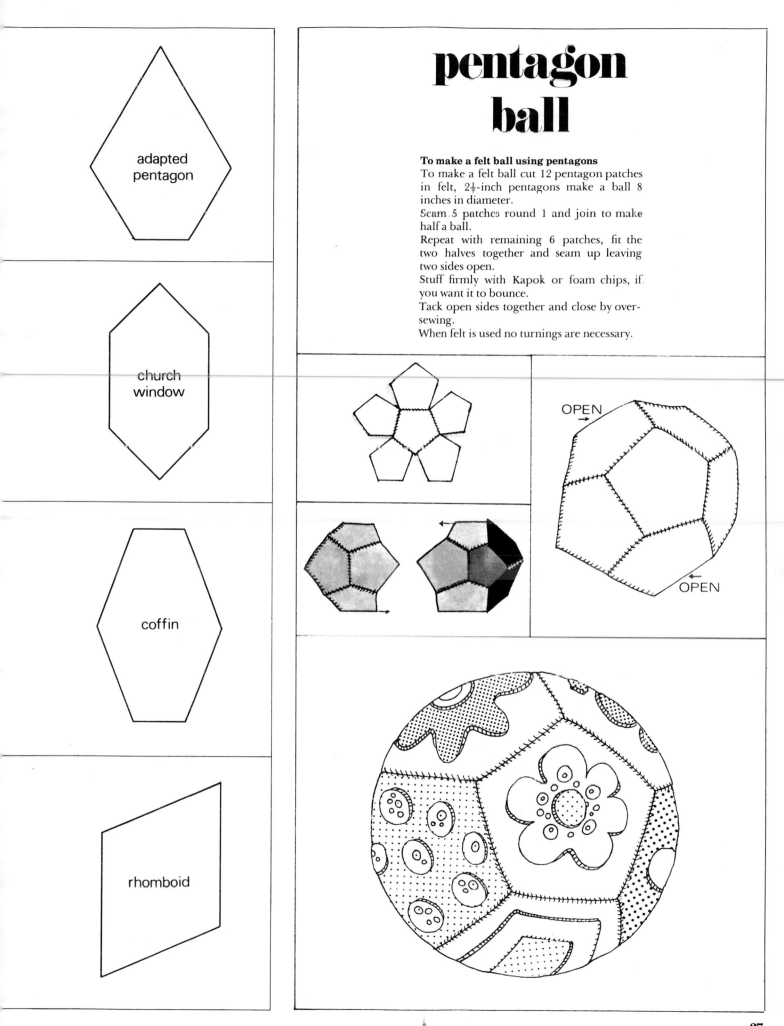

adapted
pentagon

church
window

coffin

rhomboid

pentagon ball

To make a felt ball using pentagons

To make a felt ball cut 12 pentagon patches in felt, 2½-inch pentagons make a ball 8 inches in diameter.

Seam 5 patches round 1 and join to make half a ball.

Repeat with remaining 6 patches, fit the two halves together and seam up leaving two sides open.

Stuff firmly with Kapok or foam chips, if you want it to bounce.

Tack open sides together and close by over-sewing.

When felt is used no turnings are necessary.

OPEN

OPEN

combined shapes in patchwork

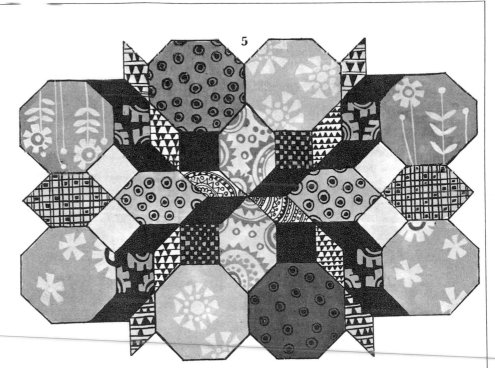

5

1. *Adapted rectangular shapes used with squares and octagons*

2. *Design made with diamonds and hexagons*

3. *'Pineapple' variation of Log Cabin with strips of alternate light and dark colours with the strips laid diagonally across the corners on every other round. Each complete square contains four half pineapples and the pattern emerges when the squares are joined*

4. *Box and star design with a hexagon, pentagons and diamonds*

5. *Design using long hexagons, octagons, long diamonds and squares*

6. *Japanese patchwork design of adapted rectangles and triangles. Each square is composed of sixteen sections but only four shapes*

6

4

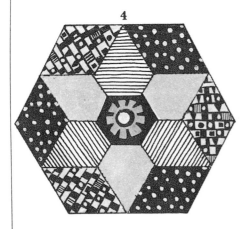

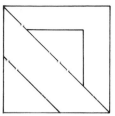

Patchwork is a very personal art — here we have a modern example. The basic block is made from a dark blue square on to which are stitched one yellow trapezoid and two triangles — one red and one multi coloured. The way in which the squares are stitched together forms the design and there are many variations. Shown below are other ways of using the same shapes

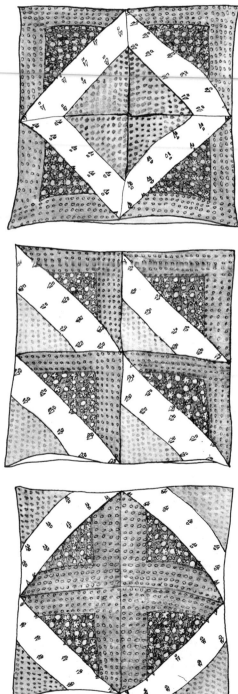

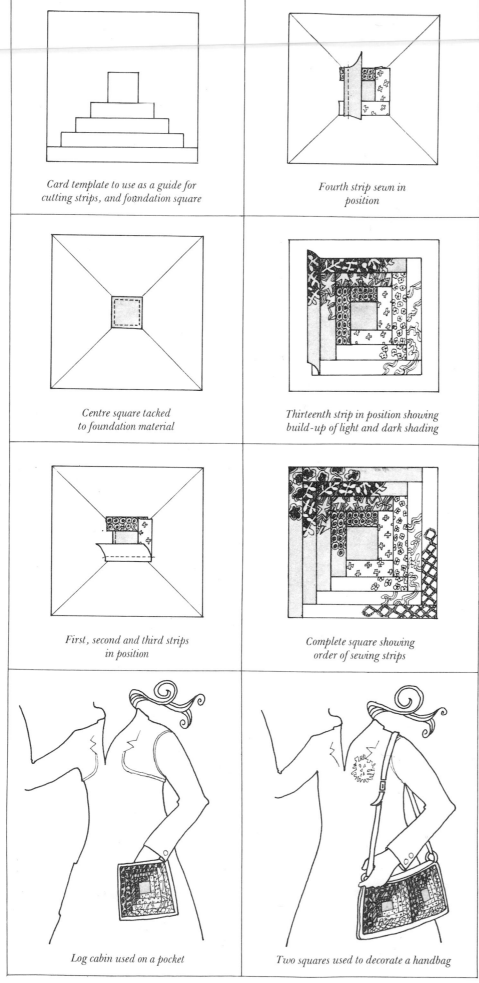

Card template to use as a guide for cutting strips, and foundation square

Fourth strip sewn in position

Centre square tacked to foundation material

Thirteenth strip in position showing build-up of light and dark shading

First, second and third strips in position

Complete square showing order of sewing strips

Log cabin used on a pocket

Two squares used to decorate a handbag

log cabin

'Log Cabin' was a popular form of patchwork both in England and America during the second half of the nineteenth century. Strips of material are built out from a central square, their edges overlapping. The square is divided diagonally by the light and dark shading of the strips. Traditionally the central square represents the fire, the light half of the square is the firelit side of the room and the dark side in the shadows.

Like crazy patchwork, 'Log Cabin' is sewn on to a foundation material so a mixture of fabrics is possible, but the design relies for its effect on the light and dark shading of the patches. Variations of this form such as 'Straight Furrow' and 'Barn Raising' depend on the placing of the light and shade patches when they are joined together. 'Pineapple' pattern is made in the same way as 'Log Cabin' except a strip is sewn diagonally across the corners on alternate rows.

To make 'Log Cabin'

You will need a square of fabric to use as a foundation – a 12 inch square is a good size if you are making a bedcover, a 6 inch if you are making pieces to make a cushion or handbag. Take a square of fabric for the centre and tack it to the foundation (see drawings). The other fabrics, in light and dark shades should be cut into strips of 1 inch wide. For each square of the design you will need two light and two dark strips.

It is helpful in placing the patches if a light pencil line is drawn diagonally from each corner of the foundation piece, crossing in the centre of the square, before the centre square is stitched into position.

The first short strip of light material is placed right side down on the centre square and stitched $\frac{1}{4}$ inch from the edge, covering one side of the square. It is then folded back and pressed down. A second strip of light material is sewn along the second side of the centre square, overlapping the first strip at one end. The third and fourth sides of the square are covered with strips of dark material, each one overlapping the previous one at the end. By using two strips of light fabric and then two strips of dark you will end up with all the dark 'logs' on one side of the square and all the light 'logs' on the opposite side.

Detail of Log Cabin (above) showing choice of flowery cotton fabrics in browns and golds

Log Cabin is used to upholster the back of a day bed and make a matching cover and pillow (right)

crazy patchwork

Crazy patchwork originated as the most thrifty way of using up even the smallest scraps of material that were useless for anything else. The scraps are stitched to a foundation material which strengthens the work.

It is possible, though not advisable, to mix different types and thicknesses of fabric in one piece of work. Early examples of crazy patchwork were made from woollen scraps to make warm blankets but the Victorian crazy work reflects the fashions of the age and were made from a mixture of velvets, silks and satins.

Crazy quilts, like the famous Jenny Jones coverlet which won a competition in Chicago in 1884, were often made in nine large blocks which were then sewn together into one piece. This particular one was edged in dark green velvet and decorated with ribbon rosebuds and forget-me-nots.

In theory it may seem easy to stitch random scraps together, but in practice it needs a good eye to arrange the pieces so they fit together well. The balance of light and dark pieces has to be considered as well as the relative sizes and shapes. The best way to start is to experiment – trim the fabrics to a suitable size and just move them around on the foundation material until you have found a pleasing arrangement. Even if the fabrics are mixed, they should all be clean, strong and ironed flat before you start.

To make a piece of crazy patchwork choose a cotton or soft lightweight material for the backing and cut it to the shape you want. Then, starting in one corner, take your first scrap and attach it to the foundation with a running stitch around the right angle. The next and subsequent pieces are tucked under or overlapped by ½ inch then stitched down with a running stitch which goes through all the layers of pieces and foundation material. Continue in this way until you have covered the entire foundation material or block if

you are making a quilt. The raw edges should then be finished with a single, double or triple-feather stitch worked in embroidery cotton. The Victorians with their love of ornamentation covered their crazy work with so much embroidery, beads, sequins and threads that the patchwork itself was hardly visible.

With a modern swing needle sewing machine crazy patchwork can be made up very easily. The scraps are simply arranged and pinned into place on the foundation fabric and the edges anchored with a wide zig-zag stitch.

Another advantage of crazy patchwork is that you can collect fabrics as you go along and do not need to work out patterns and quantities of fabric before you begin a design.

A tea cosy made from scraps of brightly coloured tweeds (left). The pieces are feather stitched in different coloured embroidery threads. It has a detachable cotton and plastic foam interlining

The cap and shoulder bag (above) are made of suede, velvet and tapestry pieces. The pieces have been sewn to the flap of the canvas bag in zig-zag machine stitch. The cap pattern is cut from interfacing, the pieces pinned in place and stitched. The peak is made of suede

First right-angled patch in position

Pieces in position before final stitching

Decorative feather stitching of pieces

Finished effect

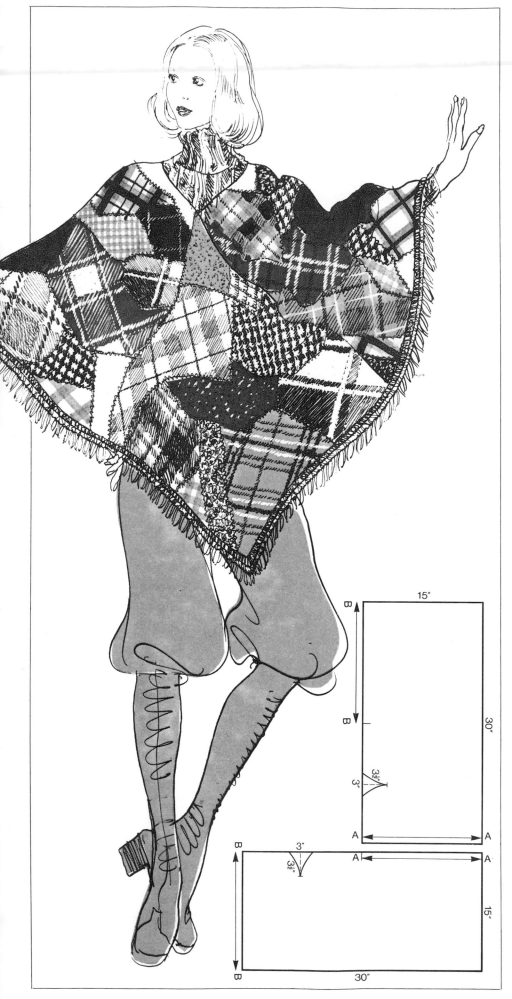

patchwork poncho

The poncho is made from two pieces of patchwork fabric 30in long and 15in wide. You will also need $2\frac{5}{8}$yd of ready-made fringing or, if you know how to make your own, you will need two balls of knitting wool and matching thread.

Making up
Take two pieces of patchwork 30in long and 15in wide.
Following the diagram, join the pieces together along AA and BB, right sides facing. Take $\frac{1}{2}$in seams and stitch to within $\frac{1}{2}$in of the neck edge.
If you want a snug fit over the shoulders, make two darts. To do this turn the garment inside out and fold as shown in the illustration. Then, at each side of the neck line where the two folds fall, make a dart 3in wide, $3\frac{1}{2}$in deep, as shown in the diagram. (Alternatively, you can underlay the neck line with straight seam tape, $1\frac{1}{2}$in shorter than the neck edge, and hold the fullness into the seam tape at the shoulders.) Press darts and carefully press the seams open.
To finish the neck edge turn raw edge under $\frac{1}{2}$in all round and hand-sew to the inside. Finish the lower edge using the same method.
Sew fringing all round the lower edge of the poncho.

Lining the poncho
If you want to line the poncho you should do this before you start to sew on the fringe. Cut the lining fabric, join AA and BB and make darts in exactly the same way as before. With right sides facing, join lining to top fabric all along the lower edge and turn it out through the open neck line. Turn in both neck edges separately for $\frac{1}{2}$in and sew the neck edges together.

Diagram for fitted poncho (left)

This crazy patchwork evening coat is particularly successful because the colours of the silk and satin pieces have been chosen so skilfully. The simple pattern was chosen and the foundation fabric cut out, tacked together and fitted. Alterations were made for a perfect fit and the darts machined. The foundation pieces for front and back were covered in crazy patchwork, finished with feather-stitching in coloured thread. The sleeves were cut from matt black satin and the whole garment was lined with black silk

clamshell

Clamshell with its semi-circular outline is one of the most difficult patchwork shapes and you need patience and concentration to master the technique. The patches are traditionally stitched together in straight rows and when finished resemble fish scales. Fabrics for clamshell should be closely woven and smooth. There are two basic ways of making clamshell patches.

The first is to cut cards and patches from templates as for other patchwork shapes. The straight grain of the fabric should run parallel to the centre of each patch. Pin a card to the right side of the patch (1). Turn down the semi-circular edge and tack round, taking tiny pleats and following the curve of the card exactly (2). The pleats must be absolutely regular with no 'pokes' to spoil the curved outline. When each patch is complete the card can be unpinned and re-used. An alternative method is to cut fabric patches from the window template as usual but use bonded fabric instead of card to make the papers. The lining is then pinned to the wrong side of the patch (3) and the curved edge is pleated and tacked as before, taking care that the tacking stitches only go through the lining material (4).

The method of joining the patches is the same for both methods. The first row of patches is laid down on a flat surface – a cork bathmat that you can stick pins in makes life easier. The top of each curve should be in a straight line and the sides should just be touching.

The next row of patches is laid in position, overlapping the first row by $\frac{1}{4}$ inch and covering the unhemmed edges. The centre of each patch in the second row should come at the join between patches in the first row. When the patches are lined up exactly you can use the solid template to check that the patches are evenly spaced. Each scallop should be the same size as the solid template. The patches should be tacked round and finally hemmed carefully round on the right side of the work. The hemming stitches should be as neat and regular as possible and should continue round the semi-circles of each line. This process of adding a row at a time is continued until the fabric reaches the required size.

There is another, more recent, method of joining clamshell patches which gives a curious meandering effect:
use templates to cut shapes from vilene and fabric patches as for other shapes. Pin the vilene to the fabric patch (5) and turn down a hem on *all* sides of the patches (6–8). The convex edges will need the material to be clipped slightly so it will ease round the curves. Join the first two patches by the tiny stem, right sides of the patches together (9). The next pair of patches are fitted into the semi-circular space and joined with a close slip stitch (10) which should not be visible on the right side of the work.

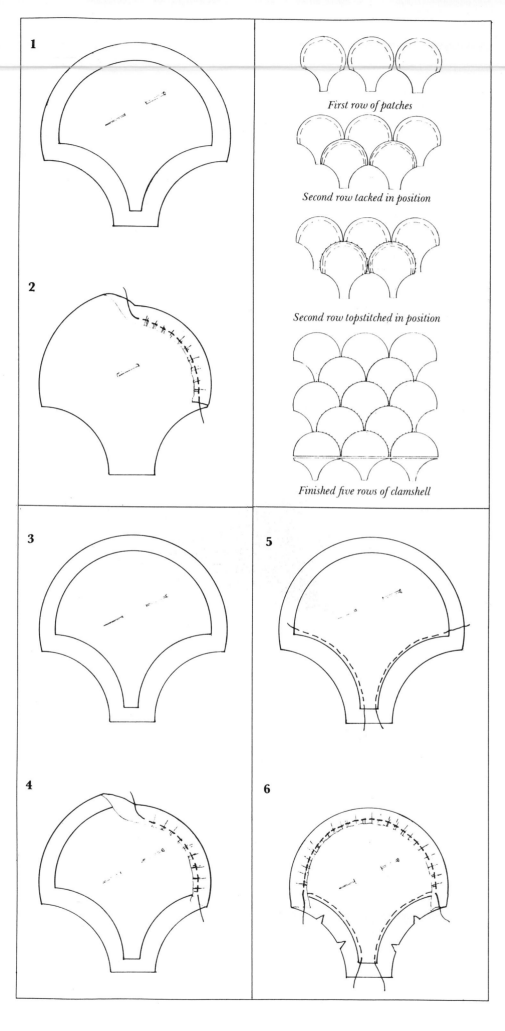

First row of patches

Second row tacked in position

Second row topstitched in position

Finished five rows of clamshell

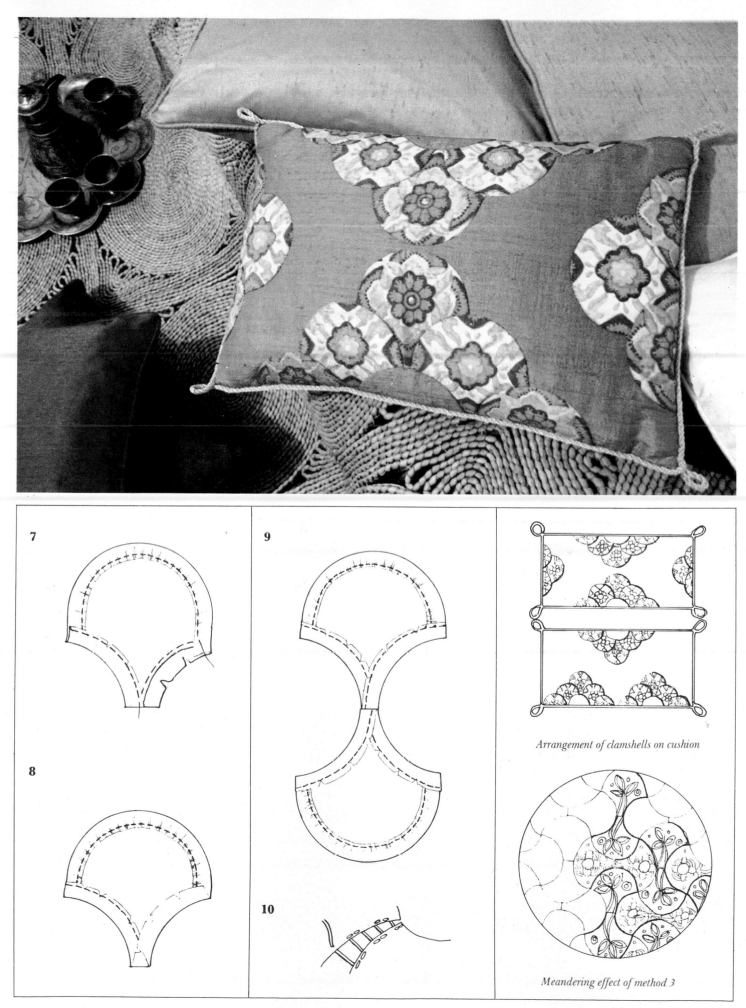

7

8

9

10

Arrangement of clamshells on cushion

Meandering effect of method 3

Simple top for a child made in fine woollen fabric worked in rows of clamshell. The number and size of the patches should be adapted to fit. Strips of matching fabric or ribbon make the halter straps and back ties

The clamshell tea cosy (below left) is designed in a 'V' shape and the hem is finished with a straight edge

Other uses of clamshell (right) are as a choker, a belt, a pocket and a housecoat trimmed with clamshell on collar, cuffs and skirt. Other ways of arranging the clamshell patches are shown below

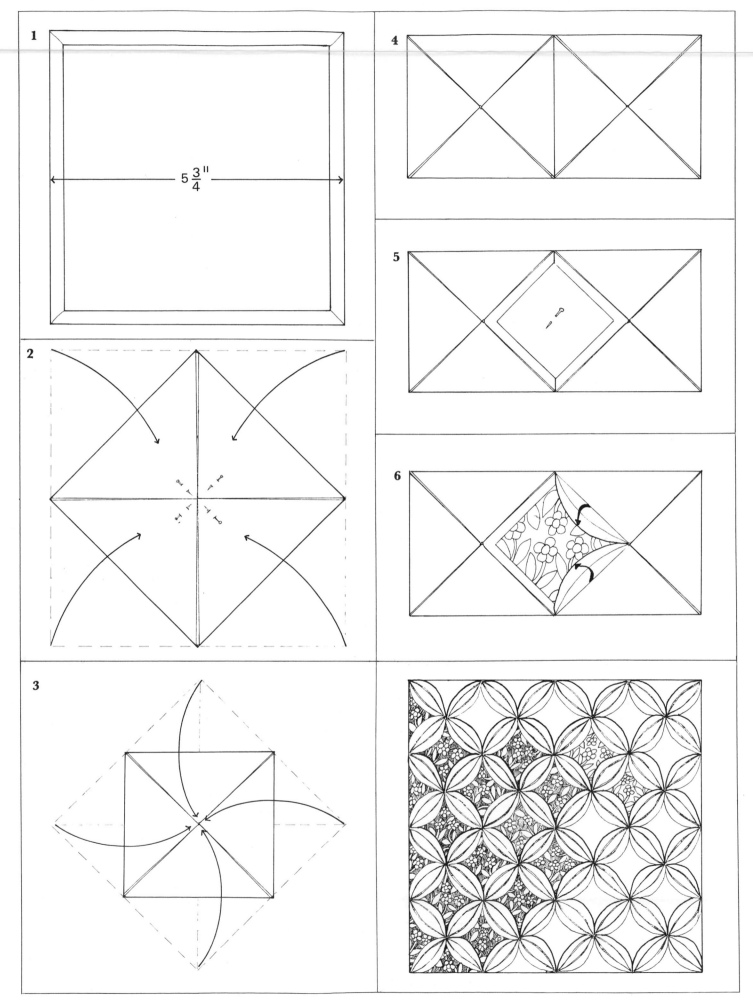

1

$5\frac{3}{4}''$

2

3

4

5

6

42

cathedral window patchwork design

This modern American patchwork pattern looks complicated but is in fact surprisingly easy to construct. The almost three-dimensional effect is achieved by folding and stitching the basic fabric over small inset squares of bright, printed cottons. The process involves several thicknesses of fabric so it is important that the basic material is soft but folds easily in the hand, a cotton such as calico is ideal. This system has the great advantage that the finished patches are complete and need no further lining.

Making the patches – see diagrams

1 Cut out a 6 inch square of calico or other soft cotton on the straight grain of the fabric. Fold down narrow turnings. The sides of the square should now measure $5\frac{3}{4}$ inches.

2 Fold each corner of the square to the centre and pin in position. The square now measures 4 inches.

3 Fold each corner of this square to the centre and pin, removing each of the first pins in turn. The square now measures $2\frac{3}{4}$ inches.

4 Make another square in the same way and join the two together.

5 Cut out a $1\frac{3}{4}$ inch square of coloured cotton on the straight grain of the fabric and pin it carefully in position over the seamed edge of the two squares.

6 Take the folded edge of the calico and turn it back over the edge of the coloured square, holding it in place between thumb and first finger of the left hand. Stitch it down with even running stitches taken through the coloured patch and the two thicknesses of calico to the back of the fabric. Make two small stitches across the calico at each corner to give a firm finish.

The edges of half-squares should be turned in and overstitched when they come at the edge of an article. The finished patchwork should not be pressed as it may lose some of its texture by doing so.

Two different versions of 'Cathedral Window' pattern, one with a light background and one with a dark. A random choice of fabric in the 'windows' gives yet another effect

suffolk puffs

This is also known as the 'Yorkshire Daisy' and the 'Puff Ball'. In America it is called the 'Yo Yo'.

As shown in the diagram, the circles (about saucer size) are drawn and cut out. The edges are turned down on to the wrong side and gathered with running stitch and drawn up as tightly as possible. The result is flattened and pressed down.

These double circles are then joined firmly as indicated to make up the required area and then lined.

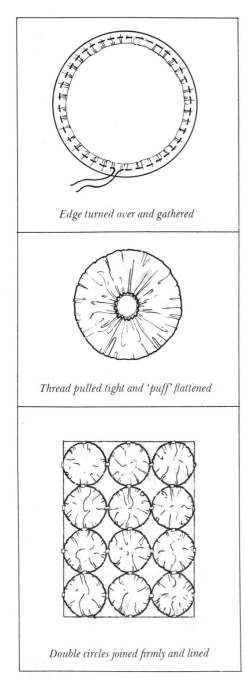

Edge turned over and gathered

Thread pulled tight and 'puff' flattened

Double circles joined firmly and lined

Shawl diagram. Cut out circles for fabric 5½ inches diameter, make ½-inch turning and gather. Sew circles together as shown to make a shawl 5ft wide and 2ft 7 inches deep

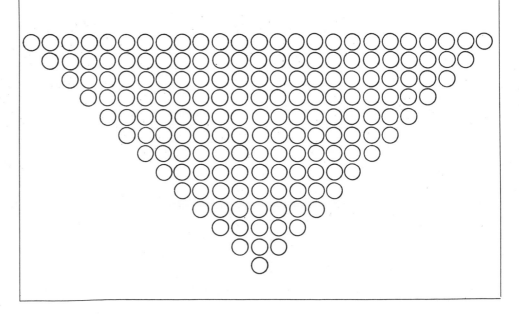

padded patchwork

Padded patchwork looks soft and luxurious and, with a sewing machine and Dacron or foam plastic filling, can be made quickly and easily.

There are two ways of making padded patchwork. The first is to make a series of separate pillows that are individually filled and then sewn together. The second is really a form of quilting, except that the lining is much fatter. Padded patchwork is usually made in squares or rectangles but if you are enthusiastic there is no reason why a large hexagonal or octagonal template could not be used just as well.

Method 1

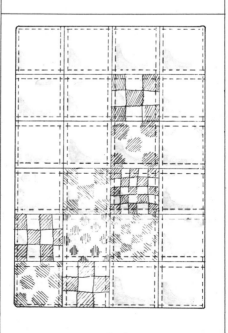

Method 2

Method 1

Draw a scale plan of what you intend to make on a piece of graph paper. Count the number of patches you need and cut twice this number of fabric patches. The advantage of this method is that it produces a finished piece of work that requires no further lining. Cut the filling into the same shapes as the patches, including the allowance for turnings, to give the finished patch extra puffiness.

Place two patches together, right sides facing and machine round on three sides. If your patches are hexagons or octagons machine round all but two of the faces. Turn the patch right side out and press seams. Insert the padding, turn in the edges of the open sides and tack. Then either top stitch by hand or with the zipper foot of the machine make a line of straight stitching very close to the edge.

When you have made up all the little cushions in this way they can either be hand-stitched neatly together or butted up and stitched with the zig-zag stitch of the machine.

An unusual way of joining the patches is to join them only at the corners, or in the case of the square at the corners and at the mid-point of the sides. These points can be decorated with tufts of cotton or with embroidered flowers.

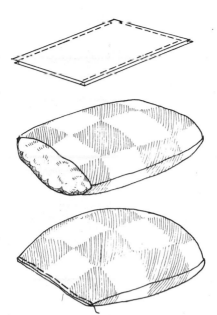

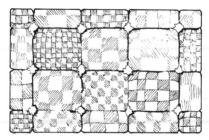

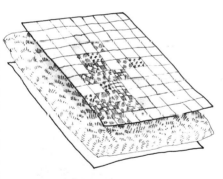

Method 2

For this method you will need fabrics to make the patchwork top, (these can of course be appliquéd or pierced patches); fabric for lining; a piece of dacron wadding or plastic foam approximately 2 inches larger than the finished work.

Machine or hand stitch the patches together to make the top. Press on the right side and remove paper shapes if you have used them. Cut lining fabric to the same size as the top and cut wadding or plastic foam 2 inches larger than the top all round.

Place the lining fabric right side down and cover it with wadding. Pin patchwork fabric on to the first two layers with right side up. Starting in the centre make long tacking stitches through all three layers (see diagram). Tack round the outside about $2\frac{1}{2}$ inches from the raw edge. If necessary trim away excess filling.

Stitch by machine (about 8 stitches to the inch) through all layers to outline shapes.

A nice rolled edge is made by leaving the outer patches unstitched.

Turn in 1 inch of the top and lining and topstitch the two edges together to finish.

Place fabric over wadding

Long tacking stitches through all three layers (below), starting from the centre

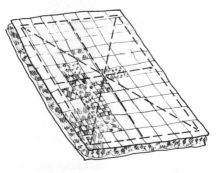

Here the bedspread and floor cushion
are made by method 2 (see previous page)
in padded patchwork. The bolster
cushions are in plain patchwork and the
small cushions repeat the fabric used in
these various patchwork items

Heavenly Steps pattern composed of rhomboids and squares

Rhomboids in 'pleated' border

Faceted octagon

Simple triangles cut out of striped fabric

Star made with tapered diamonds

design, colour and texture in patchwork

Patchwork has always been much more than a way of using up odd scraps of material. It was, and still is, a valuable form of artistic expression. Think of your fabrics and needles as an artist would consider his palette and brushes.

Having mastered the basic skills of cutting and stitching you will certainly want to experiment with shapes, colours and textures. If you see a pattern that interests you make it up into a small piece. It can always be made into a small object or cushion top and need not be wasted. It is well worth buying or making a whole set of templates so that you can experiment with lots of different shapes and choose the one, or combination, that you like best.

Collect as many fabrics as you can. Nothing is more stimulating to good patchwork design than a wide choice of fabrics of all colours and textures. Swap fabrics with your friends or buy $\frac{1}{8}$ or $\frac{1}{4}$ yards—stores are usually very good about selling small quantities and remnants for patchwork.

Colours play an important part in the design of patchwork and it helps to understand the principles of colour relationship.

The primary colours are red, yellow and blue from which all other colours are combined.

Secondary colours are made by mixing primary colours. For example, blue and yellow mixed in equal parts make green. Different shades of green can be made by varying the proportion of blue and yellow in the mix. The lightness or darkness of a colour is its tone.

Closely related colours make very pleasing patchwork designs. If you choose blue, for example, you could use a variety of tones from sky blue to navy, all the tones of green and the shades of turquoise made by mixing blue and green together.

Many of the best patchwork designs are worked in two colours only, one light and one dark. White or natural is an obvious choice of background for strong blues, greens or reds, but a subtle choice would be a light and dark shade of the same colour.

Colour can be used to make exciting three-dimensional effects. One of the simplest is the box pattern formed from three diamonds (see the album cover in the section on diamonds).

A square divided into four triangles can appear to come towards you in points if the triangles on one side are highlighted more strongly than others.

A stunning effect can be made with octagons if they are divided as shown in the drawing. Use tones of one colour with the lightest or darkest in the centre and the whole shape will appear to be faceted like a precious stone, especially if it is made in silk. A triangle divided in the same way will give a similar effect.

As the rhomboid shape is a parallelogram it can be used to give a design perspective. Here are some examples—the simplest is the border, made with pairs of rhomboids in light and dark shades, which gives a pleated effect. Rhomboids and squares used together make another variation of the box design which was traditionally called 'Pandora's box' or the 'Heavenly Steps'.

In all three-dimensional work the effect is heightened by using a striped fabric to run along the lines of the perspective.

Mixing textures is a good way of adding interest to a simple design or colour scheme. Some early examples of designs worked on a white background had patches cut from different white damasks. The difference in the texture produced a slight variation of shade. If you take a patch in blue velvet it will look glowing and jewel-like whereas a patch in exactly the same colour but in a shiny material will look much lighter and brighter. Exciting designs can be made from a mixture of silk, velvet, corduroy, tweed and satin, all in approximately the same colour. Do not plan to give an item made in mixed weights of fabric very hard wear as the heavier fabrics will tend to pull and damage the lighter ones. The difference in weights can be made up by using a bonded paper lining, but even so a mixture of fabrics will never be very strong.

Trellis design

Rhomboids and triangles

Squares of striped fabric

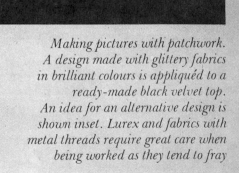

Making pictures with patchwork.
A design made with glittery fabrics
in brilliant colours is appliquéd to a
ready-made black velvet top.
An idea for an alternative design is
shown inset. Lurex and fabrics with
metal threads require great care when
being worked as they tend to fray

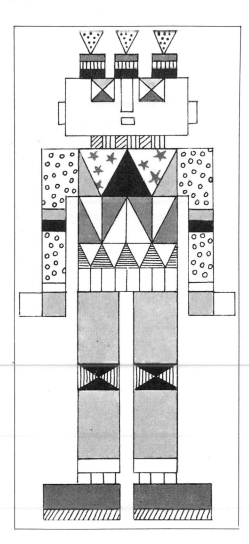

patchwork pictures

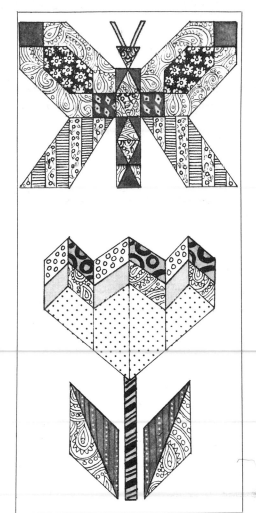

Creating pictures from traditional patchwork shapes is very satisfying. Somehow the limitations imposed by the shapes are more challenging than free patchwork, which we will talk about later. Once interested in this aspect of patchwork you will start to see things around you in terms of patchwork shapes: rectangles, squares, triangles, rhomboids and clamshells are all good pictorial bases. You can practice by taking a coloured picture from a magazine or a child's book and trying to work it out as a series of patchwork shapes. Landscapes, particularly city or urban scenes are good to begin with.

It is important that the fabrics you use follow through the design. Try to think of the colour and texture of the material in terms of the picture you are making—green velvet makes good grass, brown tweed would make a good ploughed field, satin works well as metal or glass, a checked tweed could represent a skyscraper with lots of windows.

Here are some ideas of simple pictures to make with patchwork shapes.

Clamshell patches in various sizes cut from different white cotton fabrics could make the shape of a puffy cloud. Stitch it to a blue backing and add another large yellow patch and you have the sun.

appliqué and collage

While traditional patchwork is experiencing a great revival, the same thing cannot be said for its twin sister, traditional appliqué. Perhaps it is because patchwork is essentially portable whereas appliqué, which relies heavily on quilting for its finished effect, needs to be done by hand in large pieces or on a machine. Whatever the reason it is rare today to find appliqué work of the standard achieved in the American marriage quilts of the mid-19th century. A superb example of this is the Baltimore Bride's quilt on view at the American Museum at Claverton Manor near Bath, England. It is 10 feet 6 inches wide and is made up of 25 panels, each with a different flower arrangement. The design, stitching and colours are beautiful.

Appliqué is an example of a craft that has been adapted and modernized. Machine stitching has superseded handworked blanket or herringbone stitch as it is much quicker and can look just as good. Appliqué in the form of fabric pictures, collage and creative embroidery are more frequently seen than the traditional designs of the past.

The word 'appliqué' comes from the French verb 'appliquer' meaning to put or lay on. In needlework this term is used to describe cutting one fabric to shape and sewing it on to another fabric, often with a decorative stitch.

Various methods of stitching can be used:
1. Blind hemming by hand
2. Machine stitching close to the edge using a zipper foot
For both of these methods you must allow a small hem on the cut-out piece which must be notched and turned under before stitching.
3. Herringboning
4. Buttonhole or satin stitching
5. Zig-zag stitching on a machine
For these methods the piece should be cut to the exact size, the raw edges are then covered by the decorative stitching.

Whichever method of applying the design you choose, the shape must be cut out carefully, pinned into position on the foundation fabric and tacked round with small stitches close to the edge. It must lie absolutely flat against the background. The tacking stitches should be removed except in the case of buttonhole, or satin, stitch when the stitching itself will cover them.

To make a quilt in a traditional appliqué design you will need enough background fabric to cover the bed. Traditional fabrics are white or bleached calico. It is possible to use ready-made cotton quilting for the background fabric but the design of the quilting must complement the shapes of the appliqué.

Decide on the design you intend to use. For something large like a quilt the time spent in planning is very valuable and it is worth cutting out a variety of appliqué shapes until you have found an arrangement that pleases you. When you have, cut out enough of the shapes in brown paper to complete one quarter of the quilt so you can really see what the finished piece will look like. Fold the background fabric into quarters and mark the fold lines with tacking to get the size accurate. You can copy an old design by eye or, if you have a small illustration you can enlarge it by placing a grid over it and copying the exact content of each square to the corresponding square of a grid drawn to the size of the final design.

To make up the patchwork you will need:
fabrics for the appliqué
matching thread
a fine needle
abrasive paper (medium coarse)
old scissors to cut the abrasive paper
sharp scissors to cut the fabric
Draw or trace the shapes you have chosen on to the smooth side of the abrasive paper. Cut out the shapes and place them rough side down on to the fabric. The abrasive paper will cling and help you to cut accurately. Unless you wish to centre a particular part of a patterned fabric, place abrasive paper on the wrong side of the fabric as it may be too rough for delicate fibres. Cut accurately round the edge of each abrasive paper pattern, leaving $\frac{1}{4}$-inch seam allowance, unless you plan to finish all the shapes with a herringbone or machine zig-zag stitch. In this case, the patches should be cut to the exact size of the abrasive paper shape. Remove the abrasive paper and turn the seam allowance to the wrong side of each patch, tack the edges down carefully. Press well. Assemble all the motifs now so that the patchwork is ready to be applied to the background.

To do this you will need to tack the assembled motifs on to the background fabric in your chosen design. Make sure that they lay perfectly flat. Either sew the motifs down with a blind hemming stitch or machine running stitch close to the edge, or top stitch with herringbone stitch or machine zig-zag. When the patchwork is sewn down remove all tacking threads and press the work carefully.

To finish the quilt

Traditionally American patchwork quilts were made warmer by the addition of extra layers of fabric (often old blankets) placed between the background fabric and the lining. If you are using a ready-made quilted background material the interlining is already built-in. However, the quilting will still need to be lined.

Place the lining on to the finished cover, right sides together, and machine or hand stitch round the edges leaving an opening on one side. Turn the cover right side out through the opening and close with oversewing stitches. Catch the lining fabric all over, with tiny stitches at about 5 inch intervals.

If you have used a plain background fabric you may wish to quilt the cover.

The quilting may be done on a machine using a simple straight stitch, or by hand. If you work by hand use tiny running stitches, using a stabbing technique to make sure that all the layers are caught together. If you are using a machine loosen the tension to avoid puckering. Either way, the thread should match the background fabric.

The quilting should start from the centre and work outwards towards the edges. Outline the appliqué shapes with rows of stitches through all the layers of fabric.

Fabric collage

Fabric collage is made in exactly the same way as a paper collage except the pieces are stitched instead of stuck to the background. There is great scope for adventurous use of fabrics as the collage is meant to be looked at rather than used. Lace, buttons, beads, etc. could all be used to make rich and realistic effect.

Inlay or reverse appliqué

Inlay is not often found in patchwork as it is difficult to make with materials that fray, although the Indian women in Central America decorate their cotton weave blouses in this way. Felt is a good material to use for inlay but is not, of course, washable or hardwearing. Soft but closely woven cotton would be a good choice for something that will need to be washed.

Inlay is made by tacking several layers of different coloured fabric together. A design is cut out of the top layer revealing the layer below. You will need sharply pointed scissors to do this. Another design is cut from the next layer to reveal the layer below, and so on. Each edge should be finished with $\frac{1}{8}$ inch turning and blind hemming to the layer below. Experiment with simple shapes to begin with and restrict yourself to three or four layers of fabric.

The detail picture (right) shows how three layers of appliqué are used to form the design of this bedspread.
The red, orange and grey shapes are all cut out, allowing for turnings.
The orange shape is stitched to the red, and the grey shapes are stitched to the orange, then the whole is stitched to the white foundation fabric. This is then quilted around the edge of each motif. This motif is repeated to make the magnificent bedspread shown in the picture.
Knots of thread are used for decoration and to secure the pink layer of appliqué

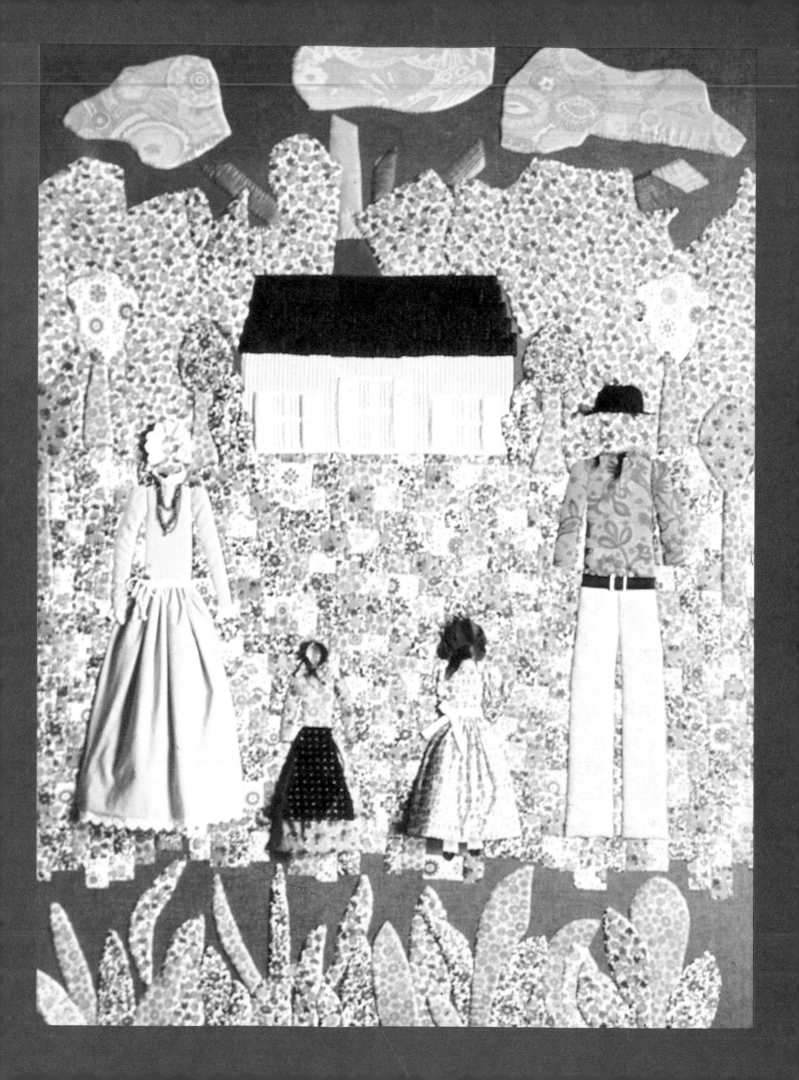

The Wall-hanging (left) is a complicated
but enchanting arrangement. The whole
design is worked on a grey background
fabric. The area behind the figures is
worked in squares of floral design with
the hedge and trees in browns and
greens. A three dimensional effect is
achieved by gathering the skirts and
adding accessories to the figures

The appliqué coverlet (above) uses
fresh clear colours to make the picture.
Rick-rack braid and tiny buttons have
been added to give definition to some
shapes and to add texture

Quilt (above) made in large squares of
padded patchwork with appliqué letters
and figures — for a child's room

The cushion (left) has an appliqué
elephant in floral print with contrasting
ears. The cushion is bordered with
matching print

The quilt (right) is made with a
traditional Sunbonnet Sue motif
appliquéd in each of the squares.
The whole quilt is lined with dark
purple fabric

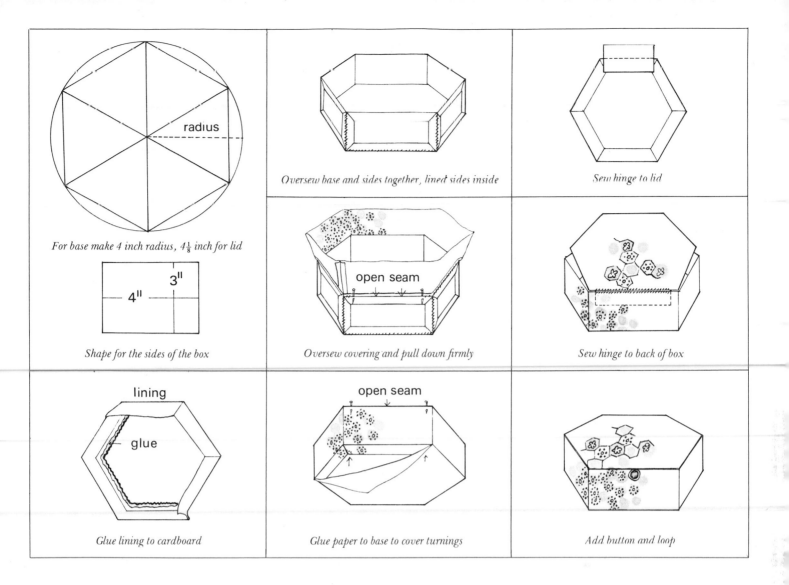

For base make 4 inch radius, 4⅛ inch for lid

Shape for the sides of the box

3"
4"

Oversew base and sides together, lined sides inside

open seam

Oversew covering and pull down firmly

lining

glue

Glue lining to cardboard

open seam

Glue paper to base to cover turnings

Sew hinge to lid

Sew hinge to back of box

Add button and loop

making boxes

Making and covering a box can be a very satisfying as well as useful way of using a small piece of carefully made patchwork.

To make a hexagonal box with 4-inch sides and 3 inches deep, suitable for a jewel box or sewing box, you will need:

a sharp modelling knife

a pencil and ruler

adhesive – any clear, non-staining one will do.

papers, templates and fabric to make patch-work top

fabrics for cover and lining

strong cardboard – stiff but not too thick

a fastener

some strong paper

On the stiff card draw one circle with a radius of 4 inches with a compass, mark equal segments and draw in hexagon. Repeat this with a circle of 4⅛-inch and draw in hexagon. This is for the lid of the box. 6 pieces of card 4 inches x 3 inches are needed for the sides of the box.

With the modelling knife and a ruler cut out these shapes.

Place hexagons and side pieces on lining fabric and draw round with a pencil. Cut out the lining allowing ½ inch turning all round. With the right side of the fabric down, lay each piece of card down on lining pieces. Squeeze a line of glue round the edge of each card shape, bring lining firmly over and stick down, folding the corners as if you were making a patch. Be careful that there are no wrinkles on the right side. Line all 6 sides of the box, botton and lid in this way. When the glue is dry, with the lined sides inside, oversew base and sides together.

Cut a strip from the cover material 24½ inches long by 4 inches wide. Check the length round the box – it should fit tightly. Seam the two ends together and press.

Turn down ⅓ inch on the joined strip and press. Pin into position round the upper edge of the box so that the wrong side is facing out and the right side of the fabric is towards the lining. Place the seam on a corner. Mark with a pin a distance of ½ inch from each corner on one side of the box, adjacent to the seam. This space will be left open for the hinge to be slipped in. Over-sew the covering all round the top edge, then turn over and pull down firmly to cover the outside of the box. Keep the fabric taut and stick the turnings down on to the under-side of the box.

Cut out a 4-inch hexagon shape from the strong paper and stick it over the bottom of the box to hide the turnings.

To make the hinge and cover the top of the lid, first cut a strip of the covering material 1½ inches wide and 8 inches long. Join on the wrong side, press seam and turn right side out. Stick this to the lid on top of the turning of the lining.

Measure the patchwork cover against the lid, turning in the raw edge. Tack round and pin to the lid then oversew all round, including across the hinge.

Tuck end of hinge into the open back of the box and oversew. Open the box lid and oversew the hinge inside.

Make a small loop of fabric and stitch to the lid front and sew a small button to the front of the box.

This basic method can be used for making and covering square and circular boxes.

Separate lift-off lids can be made in the same way with sides of only ½ inch.

Hexagonal box with a lift-off lid with the top worked in tiny hexagons in different fabrics in shades of grey (opposite page)

traditional patchwork designs

Dresden Plate
This design is based on sections of a circle, with a
circle in the centre sewn on last to cover the raw
edges of the segments
The 'Plate' part may be made by the pressed
patchwork method – as in Log Cabin – or in separate
patches oversewn together and stitched on to a
foundation fabric

Moon over the Mountain

This is an example of a three-patch block. It should be made in three different fabrics of light medium and dark tones — the moon being the lightest, the mountain the darkest and the sky the medium tone. The triangle and the circle combination is simple but effective

Windmill

This is a simple pattern based on the half-square triangle. The light and dark triangles are stitched together to form small squares. The Windmill effect comes when the triangles radiate from the central point of the square. Windmill blocks can be alternated with plain squares

The Basket

Made from long triangles with a separate appliqué handle, baskets are usually made separately and then stitched to the background fabric. Many examples of old basket quilts exist and most of them have plain dark coloured baskets — red, blue or green, on a cream calico background

The Roman Square

Some other names for this design are Beggars' Blocks and Cats and Mice. This is a nine-patch block pattern and the small squares are each made from two dark strips on either side of a lighter one. The squares are stitched together so the stripes are alternately vertical and horizontal

Grandmother Fan

The curve of the fan looks best on a medium tone background fabric. The patches of the fan can be joined together and then stitched to the background, or the fan can be made by the 'pressed' method used to make Log Cabin — one patch stitched and overlapping the next on the background fabric

Robbing Peter to pay Paul

An old Quaker pattern based on a light and dark square with circular pieces cut out of two opposite corners. This pattern is usually made in two colours. A simple version of this pattern is called Drunkard's Path and yet another version is Steeplechase

Flying Geese

You may see this called Flock of Geese or Goose Tracks. The pattern combines isosceles triangles with stripes of contrasting fabric. The small and large triangles are stitched together into strips and the quilt is always made up with the apex of the triangle pointing towards the head of the bed

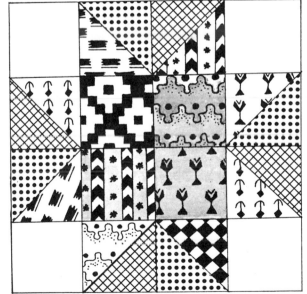

Saw-toothed Star

This pattern originated at the beginning of the nineteenth century on the east coast of America and is also called the Single Star. The pattern is made from squares and the eight points of the star are formed by half-square triangles radiating out from the central four squares of solid colour

The Wedding Ring

*This shows two methods — the interlacing method is
the more traditional design and the
overlapping is a more recent design. The sections
of the circle should be uniform in size and the
ring is always made of a variety of
patterned fabrics. The sections are oversewn
together and when completed the rings
are slipstitched together or hemmed to a plain
background. In the arrangement on the
left both rings are completed before being applied,
but in the second the second ring can
only be joined up after being looped through the
first. The shapes are made up in the
traditional way, using paper linings which are
removed as the appliqué is done*

World Without End

*This is a fascinating pattern whose name reflects
the religious preoccupation of many of the
early patchworkers. Its angular geometric shapes
can be given an art nouveau or modern feeling
if planned with bold prints. This and all the
traditional blocks might be used just once for a
pillow or extended as an appliqué border motif for
a dress. Or if you want variation with borders
or strips, central motifs and all over background,
they can be repeated or combined with others in
a large work to give a completely different effect
which, incidentally, you must take into careful
account when visualizing colours and fabrics*

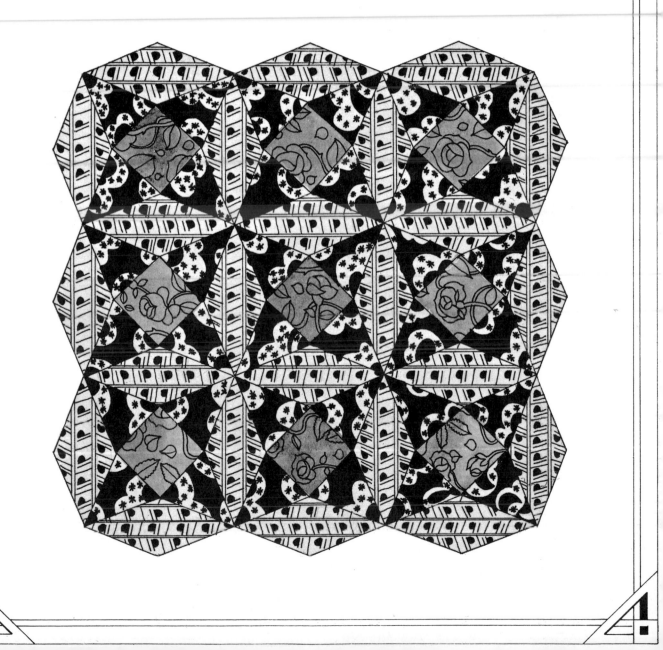

Dutch Tile

*In this easy yet effective pattern, you may use
more than two fabrics, but keep four of the
same colour together in a block with all the squares
alike except for the one which lies in the
centre of each block and this should harmonize
with the octagons around it*

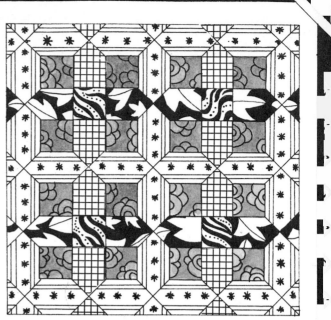

Belmont

*This design requires uniformity in fabrics throughout
and good contrast between squares and lozenges
to form the strong geometric framework. Use stripes
to advantage or embroider a linear motif on the
pointed blocks and centre square. Trace the shapes
from these blocks and enlarge as necessary*

Minton

*Another of the mosaic patterns, it calls for the
same sort-of treatment as Belmont, though
variation in fabric is possible as long as the grid
of crosses is kept consistent and a block
of lozenges is of the same cloth. The crosses look
best in plain or simply striped material*

Hesperus

*This is a handsome pattern that would be stunning
in brilliant silks. Begin by piecing small
triangles in a variety of fabrics around a large
bright octagon. Then arrange these groups,
all the same or different, among darker, smaller
octagons and light squares of repeated colour*

Variable Star

This is the foundation for so many of the star blocks. A nine-patch design of triangles and squares, it is regular enough to take some variation in fabric. For a different effect, turn it diagonally and arrange with plain cloth to form vertical bands

Clay's Choice

A four-patch block, this star is reminiscent of the Windmill in the slanting movement of the points. It's a simple enough combination of shapes but one that allows for a pleasing and clearly defined result as an all-over design or border, especially if colour patterning is regular

Falling Star

The turning motion in Clay's Choice is even more evident in this rather complex and difficult to piece combination of triangles, rhomboids and squares. To preserve its lovely effect, you must use only two definitely contrasting fabrics and a plain background and centre

Rising Star

The popular star-without-a-star motif can be extended and enlarged, radiating right to the edges of the work; or many stars might be set in a grid pattern. To vary, turn the inner star on its axis. This design works best when simple dark and light fabrics are used alternately

Virginia Star
This is one form of the popular 8-point star known
variously as the smaller Lone Star, which is
usually arranged in columns with a harmonizing
border around each, and the enlarged Bethlehem
Star, which covers the entire quilt with concentric
circles of alternating colours radiating from
the centre. Piece long diamonds for each point and
then join all points adding the outer background
pieces at the end. With any block pattern,
random colour arrangement is seldom successful —
combine colours to repeat throughout, in stripes
or squares or circles ; or if blocks vary, make
sure there is some common colour link in each

collection of quilts

Sawtooth Star
*A regular, popular block pattern, this design is
done with squares and diagonal half squares.
This fresh quilt and all but the last on the next
pages were made in America in the 19th century*

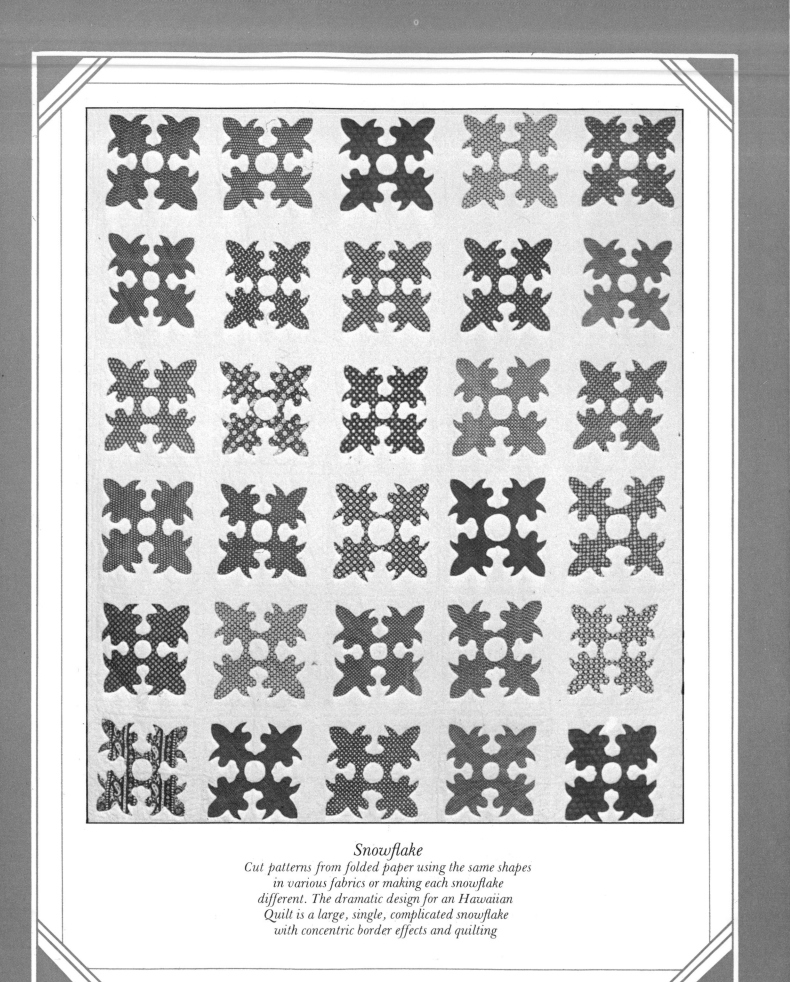

Snowflake
Cut patterns from folded paper using the same shapes
in various fabrics or making each snowflake
different. The dramatic design for an Hawaiian
Quilt is a large, single, complicated snowflake
with concentric border effects and quilting

Schoolhouses
These familiar shapes make an airy and homely
appliqué arrangement for a child's quilt,
but they would be just as charming as a border
for kitchen curtains or as a single motif
on an oven glove or napkins and placemats

Ohio Farmyard

This unusual quilt combining farm animals and machinery is a good example of how the lives of the patchworkers were reflected in their quilts. The style is somewhat crude but it is possible to embellish cutouts with embroidery, cut them from patterned fabric or combine fabrics to give realistic dimension and variety to the shape. Opposite are some of the many traditional appliqués. 1) This rather primitive tree border is one of the simpler and heartier country designs 2) Another

motif for a more elegant border is this festoon of hexagons 3) The laurel wreath makes a graceful central design with its gently curved branches 4) Hearts and Kisses (the kiss implied in the X formation) was used especially on marriage quilts. The number of appliqué designs is virtually infinite, and the objects around you will suggest other more personal possibilities. Try something as contemporary as a border of jet airplanes. After all, the original patchworkers chose motifs like the farm machinery that were, to them, quite 'modern'

Baltimore Bride

The small border detail of this lovely wedding quilt gives only a hint of its charm. Each block was worked separately and sometimes signed; then all were joined and the exquisite border added. A border is the finishing touch of any quilt; it can be a flowing and floral appliqué like the one above or geometric like those opposite. 1) This handsome border shows the corner section which must be carefully planned 2) Slanted rectangles would be effective in striped fabric 3) When stripes of Tree

Everlasting are joined, the background produces
downward pointing rows as well 4) Linked stars
are pieced from patches and then appliquéd to
background fabric 5) Cable twist gives a three-
dimensional effect if the long pieces are light and
the short ones dark 6) This combination of

squares is a versatile border or all-over pattern.
Most of the border designs can in fact be
used to form what is called a 'strip design' to make
an entire quilt. This is especially nice if
border strips are alternated with other strips or
blocks or if different colours are used in each

Princess Feather
*Here is a typically American design which takes
its inspiration from the Red Indian or,
equally, from a fireworks display. The stars and
gay fabrics complete the exotic aura lent by
the swirling configuration of the feathers*

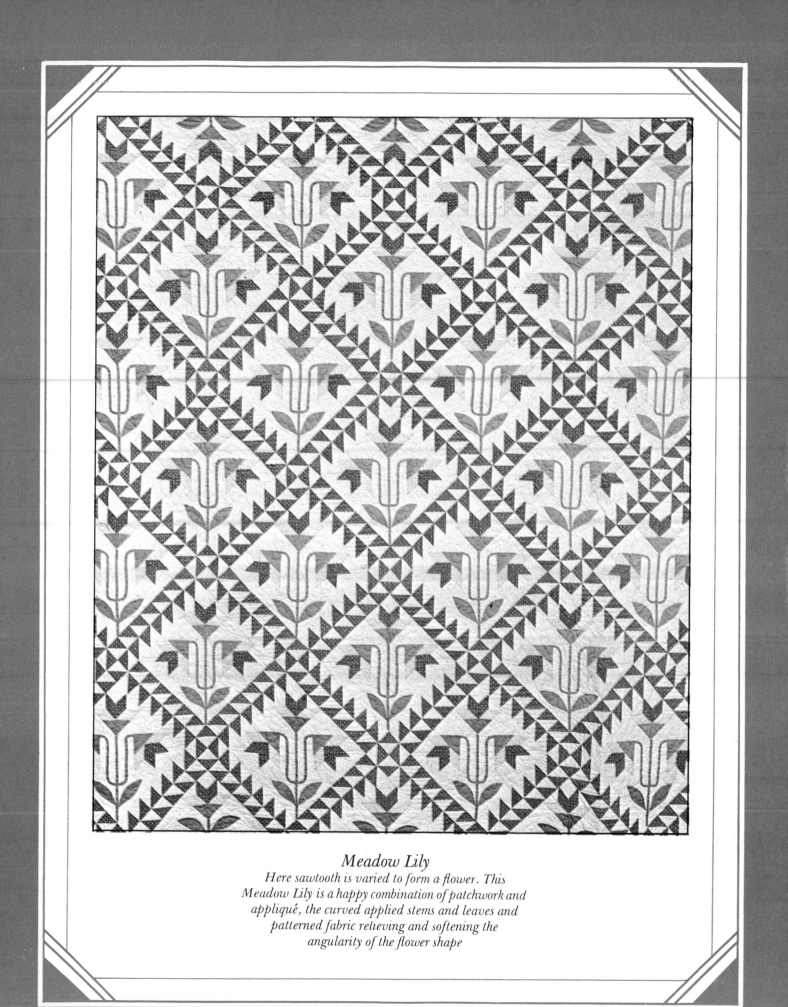

Meadow Lily

*Here sawtooth is varied to form a flower. This
Meadow Lily is a happy combination of patchwork and
appliqué, the curved applied stems and leaves and
patterned fabric relieving and softening the
angularity of the flower shape*

Cactus Flower

Another sawtooth flower quilt is enlarged to give some idea of the richness possible with quilting stitches, which usually followed the seams of the patches or covered large or unpatched areas in regular squares, diamonds or stripes. But often unpatched areas were decorated with very elaborate stitchery. 1) Princess Feather can be used as a full circle (as on the quilt illustrated) or the half-circle shown can be placed to form a curving snakelike band 2) The simple daisy is used singly

or in bunches 3) Cable stitch is good for borders. Here the corner turning is shown 4) The leaf design also works well radiating from the corners. Just as these shapes might be used as appliqués, so too might patch or appliqué motifs be adapted for quilting designs. Transfer designs onto the finished patchwork with a tracing wheel or tailor's chalk. Pin patchwork, wadding and lining to a quilting frame and quilt in one direction to avoid puckering, using small even stitches and a long sharp needle pushed straight through the fabric, not slanting or wavering

Garden Wreath

*The rounded, floral appliqué forms on this quilt
give it a lush quality which can be augmented
by padding or stuffing the shapes as they are applied,
a technique called trapunto. This might replace
or complement the more traditional quilting*

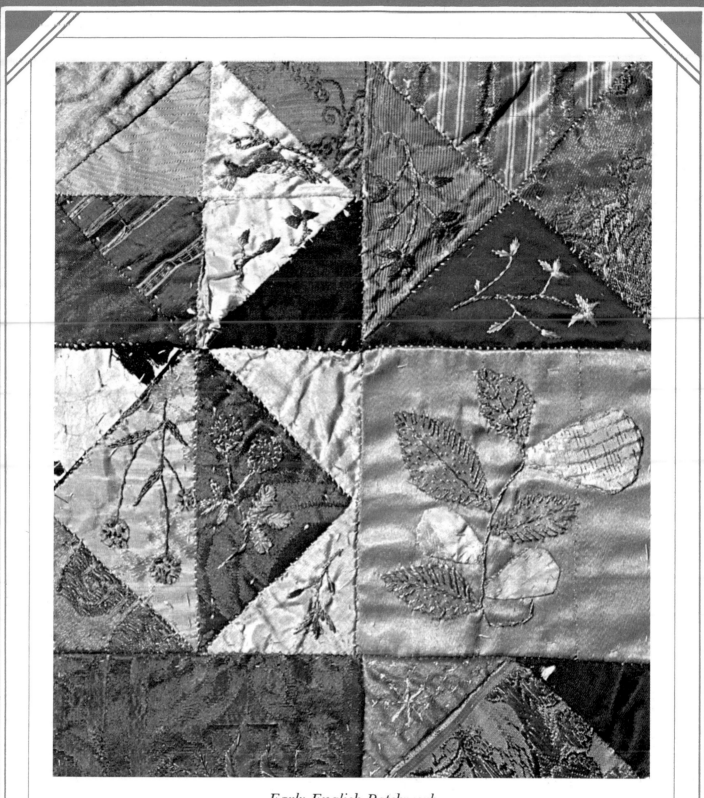

Early English Patchwork
This detail of an 18th century bedspread shows
a complex combination of embroidery and
patchwork in rich patterned fabrics. The total
effect resembles crazy patchwork in the
random, concentrated use of colour and pattern

patchwork goes Victorian

The Victorians, with their love of myriad patterns, lavish embellishment and luxurious fabrics, took naturally to the possibilities of patchwork, in fact the crazy quilt is forever associated with our Victorian grandmothers. (Oddly enough, though, crazy patchwork doesn't quilt well because the pattern of the quilting stitches following the natural seams, the only feasible way, makes a chaotic tracery on the back.) Work with brightly printed and striped silks and satins or jewel toned velvets; embroider with beads, fine silk and gold threads; add a bit of fringe or lace for the perfect evocative finish.

Delightful bijoux for yourself and your home. Stitching an exquisite capelet or dainty evening bag (above and below), a cushion that's just the right touch for a sophisticated room (left) or, most ambitious, an opulent crazy bedcover (far left) are some of the lovely ways to indulge your most sybaritic tastes : they should all gleam like precious gems

patchwork goes modern

Patchwork shows its versatility by happily adapting itself to modern dress and decor. Bold appliqué or patchwork in brilliant colours would be exciting for evening on a long swirling skirt (right). A striking background curtain of felt (far right) is made by stitching thé fluid shapes onto a backing fabric which acts as a lining as felt is apt to fade. Felt is easy to work with because it requires no turnings, but it does not wash and is not particularly hard-wearing. Take abstract appliqué shapes from modern and commercial art or fit irregular geometric shapes together to give the strong, clear lines of the lively pillow (above). Alternately, some of the traditional blocks can look very modern, especially if they are angular and if bright colours are used

town and country

Patchwork at home' in the most elegant setting (left). Plain curtains gain distinction with a border and ties of delicate design in subtly printed fine fabric. Make your own curtains or add borders to some that are ready-made. Have a whirl in this fun loving dress (right), with its pert peplum and ruffly underskirt. Adapt bright country calicoes to your favourite pattern. Here it's a simple dirndl skirt topped by a fitted, puff sleeve jacket over a separate blouse, all set off with a dark contrasting binding

A charming touch for evenings at home— make a pair of patchwork boots (below). Cut a pattern from another pair of boots, making an allowance for front and back seams. (If you want them fairly tight, insert a heavy zip up the back.) Cut soles from thick suede and punch holes at close intervals around the edges for ease in stitching to the upper portion, or you can buy soles already prepared. Position the finished patchwork fabric to best advantage when cutting the pattern; also cut a lining and stiff interlining, both $\frac{3}{4}''$ shorter at the top than the patchwork piece. Treat the patchwork fabric and the interlining as one when making up and insert the zip if you're using one; prepare the lining in the same way, making sure to clip all curved seams. Place outer boot and lining together, wrong sides facing, and tack all loose edges. Attach boot to sole, right sides facing, overcasting by hand with strong carpet thread. Neaten the top by turning the patchwork fabric $\frac{1}{4}''$ and then turning again over the lining and tacking. Finish the outside with braid or decorative binding—and some flippy tassels.

working with leather

Leather can be used successfully for really luxurious patchwork, something that would appeal especially to a man.

For most of the makes a beginner will want to attempt, sheep skin is probably the best skin to use. It is supple, easily obtainable and falls into the medium price bracket. Sheep skin is dyed to a wide variety of colours as well as being finished in attractive natural tones, and can be used for leather garments and is ideal for accessories. Sheep skin suede is of a particularly good quality, soft and velvety, and is usually used for better quality fashion clothes.

Cowhide is a much heavier leather and comes in two or three different thicknesses, the central area of the hide being the thickest. This is used for shoe soles, suitcases and anything which needs to wear well. The sides of these hides are thinner and are suitable for heavier weight garments, such as skirts and jerkins.

Cowhide is also sold in 'splits', which means that the skin has been split through its thickness into two layers. Splits are the cheapest kind of leather to buy, but are not terribly strong and shouldn't be used for articles where there is likely to be a strain on the leather—such as across the shoulders of a garment. It's perfectly suitable for accessories and is easily obtainable.

Calfskin, the smooth, beautiful leather used for good handbags and shoes, is available in different weights and finishes and is more expensive than sheepskin.

Among the fancy leathers are pigskins, goatskins, lizard and snake skin and fish skin, but these are generally rather difficult to obtain.

Leather and suede is sold by the square foot unless one is buying offcuts or scrap pieces. Skins are of an irregular shape with the legs and neck of the animal sticking out from the 'body', but these are calculated in the given measurement.

Leather or suede patchwork is an adaptation of normal patchwork because, as leather does not fray, it is possible to sew the patches together without turnings and there is no need to use papers. Simply butt the edges

This opulent bedspread is easier than it looks. Keep the shapes simple and the richness of the leathers will speak for itself. The feeling leather gives is worlds away from cotton; visualize suede hangings with primitive African motifs, a completely new dimension to traditional patchworking

of the patches together and zig-zag stitch on the right side. However, turnings can be made on thin leathers. For sewing using a sewing machine, medium thick needles will be found to be the most satisfactory, and the size of stitch should be regulated to the thickness of the leather. For thick work, set the stitch large, and for fine leather the stitch can be relatively small. Suedes tend to drag when more than one thickness is going through the machine, and to correct this adjust the stitch to the next size up. The thread will sink into the suede anyway and the finished appearance should be satisfactory.

Before you begin to sew patches together, practice on some spare scraps, you may possibly have to use a special leather needle in your machine and tissue paper under the leather.

You may also glue patches to a backing fabric, stitching later for effect if desired. There are good leather glues available in craft shops in both tubes and jars. Tubes are useful for edges and small areas; a jar with a brush is more satisfactory for larger areas. Rubber solution and latex based adhesives are good because they will rub off without leaving a stain. Glueing is mostly used for attaching lining leathers to surface leather

and for putting on decorative leather edgings and bindings.

You may be able to make the patches from leather offcuts but if using whole skins try to cut as economically as possible, avoiding blemishes. You can ignore the nap of the suede, if you cut in various directions it will add interest to the texture.

Make paper patterns of your basic patchwork shapes, secure to wrong side of skin with adhesive tape and mark round patterns with ballpoint or felt pen. Cut with very sharp scissors.

When making garments, use regular commercial patterns of a very simple shape. Either cut a heavy cotton backing fabric of each pattern piece onto which the patches are glued, or make up the patched leather 'fabric' from which the pattern pieces are then cut. Finally, make the garment as instructed in the pattern.

For a comfortable finish, line patchwork with a firm, non-slip fabric. Attach lining with a slightly different technique as you cannot slipstitch on to leather. First stitch straight tape all round inside edge of finished patchwork, press seam allowances of lining to wrong side and then slipstitch lining to tape, wrong side of lining to wrong side of patchwork.

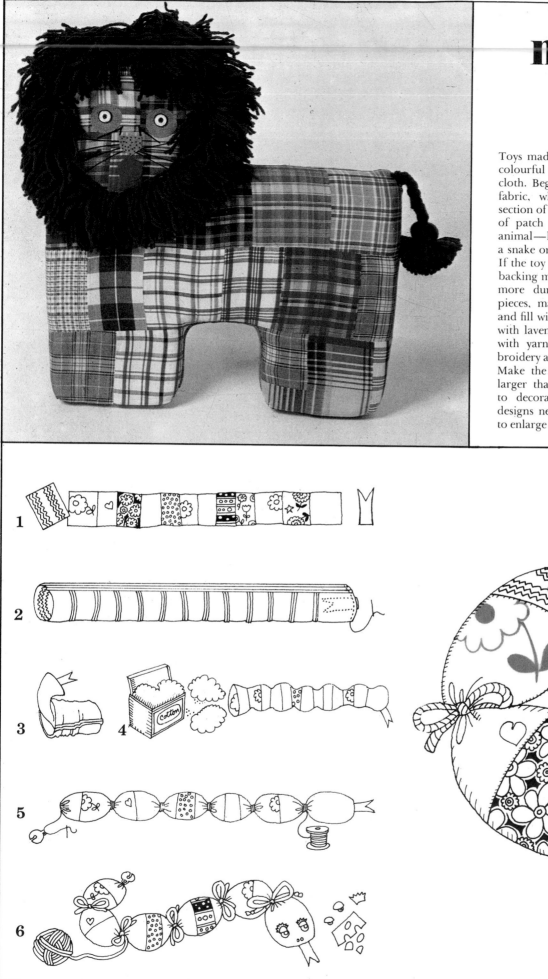

making toys

Toys made from patchwork are irresistably colourful and a good way to use small bits of cloth. Begin by making enough patchwork fabric, which may be different for each section of the animal's body. Take advantage of patch shapes that suggest parts of the animal—like using diamonds on the back of a snake or clamshell on the breast of an owl. If the toy is to get a lot of use, strong cotton backing material for each piece will make it more durable. Then simply cut out the pieces, machine stitch the shapes together and fill with wadding or, for a special touch, with lavender, pot pourri or incense. Trim with yarn, felt, buttons, ribbon and embroidery as you please.

Make the animals any size you like, from larger than life down to miniature shapes to decorate a Christmas tree. The trace designs next page are just a guide for you to enlarge or reduce.

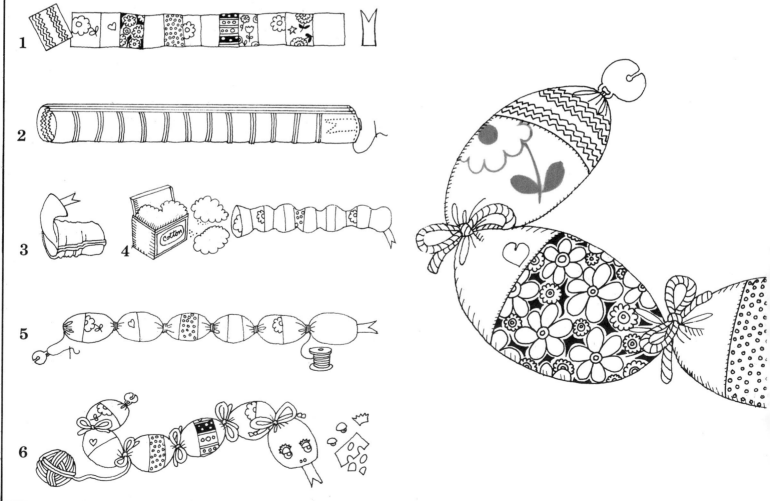

1

2

3   4

5

6

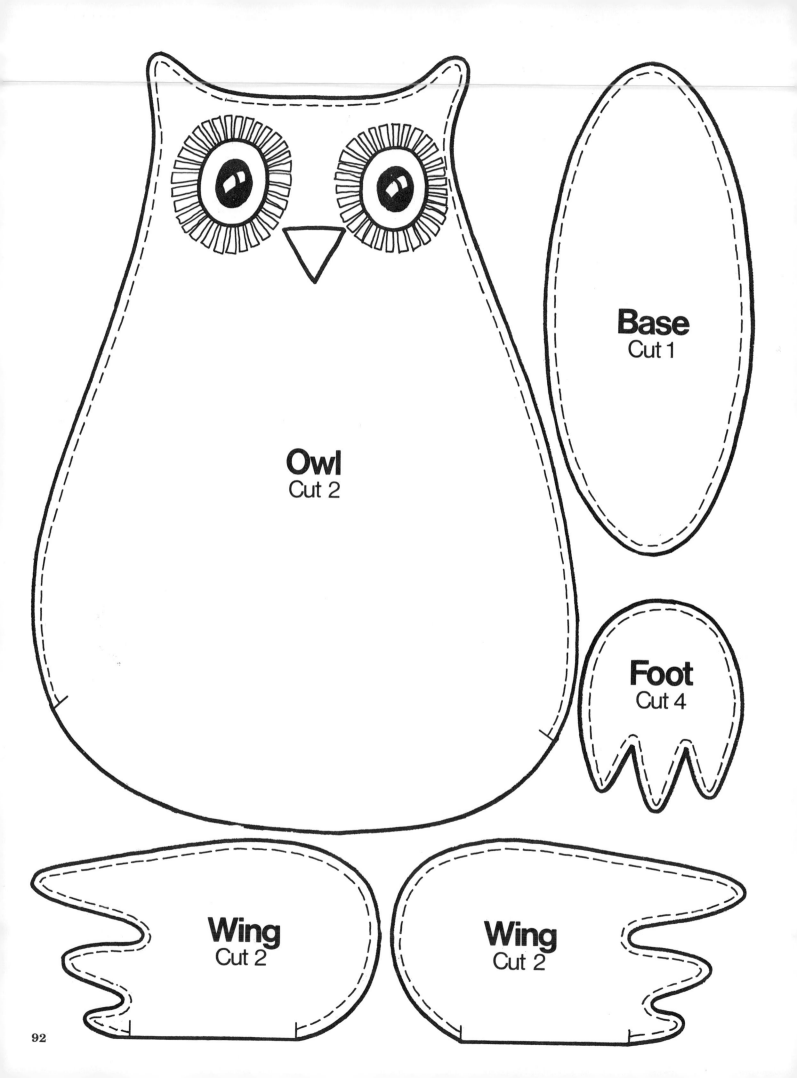

Base
Cut 1

Owl
Cut 2

Foot
Cut 4

Wing
Cut 2

Wing
Cut 2

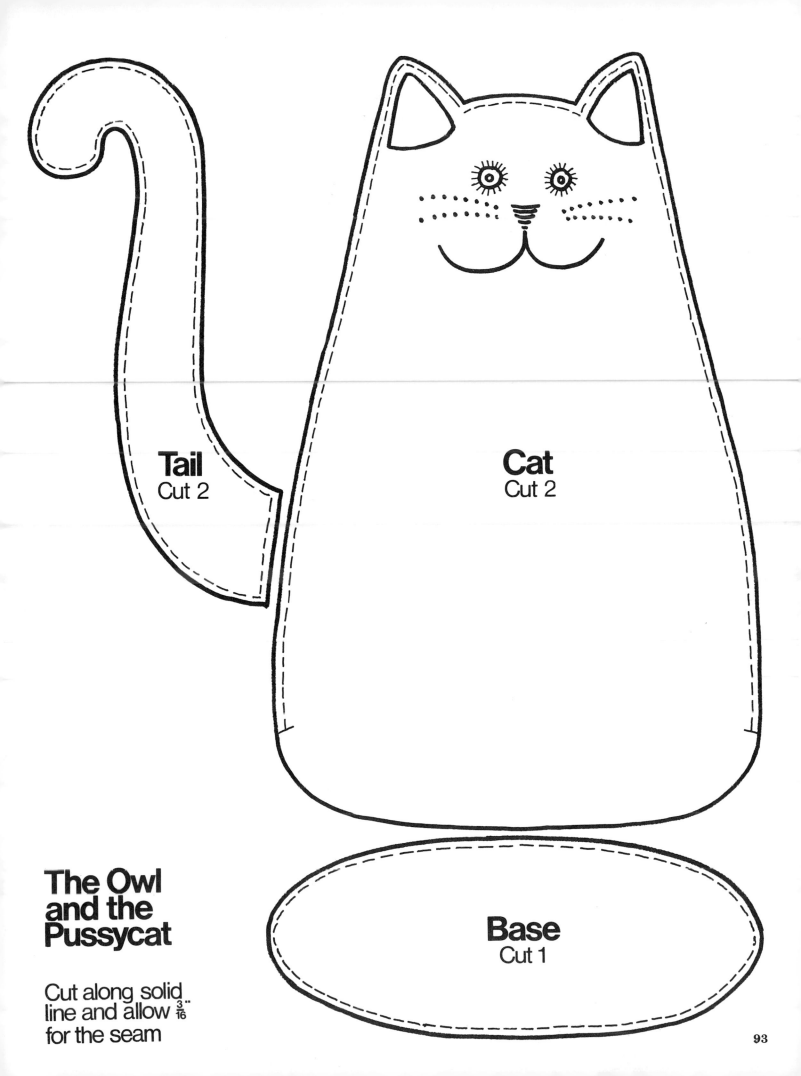

Tail
Cut 2

Cat
Cut 2

Base
Cut 1

The Owl
and the
Pussycat

Cut along solid
line and allow 3/16"
for the seam

93

whimsical bedcover

*This delightful quilt of a country scene is a
bright variation of the traditional patchwork
bedspread. Enlarge the tracing pattern in
proportion to the size quilt you want; 12"
across would be about right. Cut out each
shape of the landscape from card,
allowing for a slight turning when appliquéing.
You can calculate the amount of fabric
necessary by laying the shape several times over
½ square yard and then judging from there
how much material you will need. If you use one
of the decorative embroidery stitches shown
to apply the shapes, quilting should be kept very
simple if it is used at all*